FOREWOR

EMMANUEL KOJO H̶O̶P̶S̶O̶N̶, ̶P̶H̶D̶

𝔘𝔫𝔪𝔞𝔰𝔨𝔦𝔫𝔤

MANHOOD

*A Call to Practicing the Art of Fathering,
Fulfilling the Mandate of Manhood
&Fatherhood*

RICHARD AKITA

1

UNMASKING MANHOOD

First Printing, January, 2017

ISBN: 978-9988-2-4927-4

Unless otherwise indicated, all of the scripture quotations are taken from the Authorized King James Version (AKJV) of the Bible and New King James Version (NKJV) of the Holy Bible. Scripture quotations marked with NIV are taken from the *New* International Version of the Bible. Scripture quotations marked with NASV are taken from the New American Standard Version (NASV) of the Bible. Scripture quotations marked with Amplified are taken from The Amplified Bible (TAB).

PUBLISHED BY:

LAUNCHPAD PRESS:

CONSULTING EDITOR: CLAUDE A. MANN

COVER DESIGN: THE GRID CONCEPT

PRINTED BY: NAB SUPERIOR SERVICES

Unmasking Manhood

"The silent cries
The wetness of the pillow
Real tears guised with sweat from the sweltering heat
of a humid night with tears from uncertainty...

The silent yearn
The shyness concealing the heart cry
Opinionated views of on-lookers, yet locked in the
depth of a heart seeking approval as its coded key...

The silent admiration
The look away
Stunted by historical rejections, nonetheless, hopeful
of a word of encouragement...

The Boy — The Youth — The Man
Society demands an unwritten standard, etched on the
history laid by a bygone generation.
Family inserts foundations that are flawed
Personal expectation and devotion fraught with
identity crisis.

To unmask the man is to be the MAN!

Trapped in the body of the man is the boy wishing to
unleash the dream yet resisted by forces untold,
reprimanded by errs of forefathers.

How then can unmasking be the solution to the reality
of masked pretentious acceptance?

The journey;
The script written before birth yet influenced by living
the truth.

Unmasking manhood was never the beginning but the
demand of a role to mark the vapour of life with an
indelible impact of change.

Unmasking is the clarion call to MANHOOD".

- **RICHARD AKITA**

Endorsements

"Finally...a Male book with authentic and credible answers to the nagging questions of Manhood is birthed! These wise words will help you stand up as man in a generation struggling to protect the threatened traditional identity of Manhood and Fatherhood. Little wonder our nations are reeling in crisis. Richard has come to the rescue with this timely piece.

- **Dr Chiefo Ejiofobiri** - *President, ACE Foundation for Peace and Development and Author, Living Life by Design*

A Huffington Post story of June 13th 2014 titled *5 Lies We Should Stop Telling About Black Fatherhood* pointed out "oftentimes, when we discuss fatherhood we assume that African-American men aren't part of that conversation, largely because a number of studies and reports have repeatedly told us that black fathers are *overwhelmingly absent* from their children's lives. However, while these numbers are nothing to ignore, they contribute to a damaging narrative about black men and negate the achievements of the number of black men who play an active role in their children's lives". The story then went on to debunk five lies about black fatherhood.

There is a long-held myth that the black man suffers from habitual dereliction of duty as far as fatherhood is concerned. In fact, the United States' Center for Disease Control (C.D.C) report issued in December 2013 found that black fathers were the most involved with their children daily, on a number of measures, of any other group of fathers - and in many cases, that was among fathers who didn't live with their children, as well as those who did. I agree with the view that "it is not true that black fathers suffer a pathology of neglect" and Richard Akita's wonderful new book on the subject offers a guide and a roadmap for getting it right as a father.

Equal numbers of fathers from all races and professional backgrounds agree that it's important to be a father who provides emotional support, discipline, and moral guidance. Richard's Unmasking Manhood provides a blueprint for current fathers to learn, adjust and shape their fatherhood performance, whilst offering would-be dads the chance to prepare adequately before starting the journey. Every man must read *Unmasking Manhood!*

> - ***Michael Ohene-Effah***– *Co-Founder, LeadAfrique, Development Practitioner, Impact Entrepreneur, Youth Activist, Author, Trainer and Speaker., Accra, Ghana.*

A timely classic; a guiding light and a shepherd's staff for all those who must not just be biological fathers, but shepherds for their offspring and those that they'll be privileged to adopt. *Unmasking Manhood* is a must read!

-   **Michael Dollars** - *Speaker, Trainer, Author, Strategist: Motivation. Philosophy, Psychology.*

By God's grace and direction, I have spearheaded the advocacy of responsible manhood and fatherhood for close to two decades. I have studied the male species and the psychology of the male. The conclusion seems to suggest that many males grow from boyhood to manhood without a systematic guide that helps men understand who they really are.

Thus, our society is filled with men who are still boys in their emotions, thoughts and attitude. Strangely, almost every institution has textbooks that help in training its members, yet manhood and fatherhood are among the few institutions that lack training methods and manuals. A boy graduates into an adolescent and to a man without a training program, yet he is supposed to *'train'* his children *'the way'* they should "go".

I am therefore so gratified that author/trainer Richard Akita has penned this inspirational and insightful book, *Unmasking Manhood*. I am glad I was part of Richard's writing/editing team, and I can assure you that this is the book you have been waiting for! I can see this book in every home, church and in the libraries of many educational institutions. I recommend this book to every man, especially you! Man, you will discover and re-discover your true identity in *Unmasking Manhood*!

- ***Claude A. Mann, Snr.*** – *President, FatherServe Africa, CEO, Diamond-Pen Writings. Pastor, Nurse, Relationship Counsellor, Motivational Speaker, Author.*

Dedications

Who but you could have directed and crafted my steps, embed in me the core values of fatherhood?

Who but *you* lived and exemplified the role that I aspire to attain?

Who but you made it possible that in my weakness, your strength is displayed flawlessly?

Onto You, Heavenly Father I dedicate this book!

To my father, my hero and my coach Mr Ebenezer Laryea Akita, I dedicate this book. Thank you for allowing me to see the benefits of being your son!

Acknowledgements

I cannot talk about *Unmasking Manhood* without experiencing the full spectrum of the joy, pain, challenges, broken promises, learning opportunities, failure and successes the role demands.

To this end I thank my dear Swee: Mrs Najate Akita for giving me the opportunity to be a father; teaching me the benefits of listening and assisting me to develop the crude skills into a refined man.

To my children who tested the refinement and propelled me to strive to be better; Marcelle Akita and Ryzard Akita.

Thank You to the following who have impacted my life: -

Claude A. Mann; my Researcher and Editor

Marcelle Mateki Akita; my English Teacher

Michael Ohene-Effah; my Mentor

Patrick Otieku-Boadu; my Coach

Akwasi Marfo; my Sounding Board

Ryzard Akita; my Protégé

TABLE OF CONTENTS

FOREWORD BY

Emmanuel Kojo Hopeson, PhD

The first time I met Richard was 6th March 2016 at a Parent and Friends networking event. He simply introduced himself as Richard Akita and we shared a few fleeting words after the event. Since then, he has become one of my favourite people due in part to his affable nature, but more importantly because of his passion for Christ and his insights into family and leadership issues. Thus, this book – *Unmasking Manhood* - did not come as a surprise when he first mentioned it!

As I read the manuscript, I reckoned with myself how much fatherhood as a pillar of sound home-building has been neglected. It occurred to me over and over again how the question of fatherhood has been ignored or only partially answered. Even though there is abundant sociological research on the definition, style, approaches, and consequences of fatherhood particularly in the western world, much of this research has not tackled fatherhood the way Akita has. The central argument Richard Akita makes in this book is that **manhood is a calling** which goes beyond procreating children; he calls for fatherhood as **a position of responsibility** for men whether they are single, unmarried, divorced, or have their own children.

As a professional counsellor and conflict expert myself, I am keenly aware of the effect that the absence of fathers bring to bear on relationships. Over the years, I have dealt with psycho-social problems which can easily be traced to the dereliction of duty by fathers.

The labour that has gone into this writing is immediately apparent. Akita makes very insightful observations about fatherhood, observations which could only have come through a painstaking commitment to the subject and its varying nuances. He has carefully made available multiple approaches to fatherhood, and provided examples critical to developing self-leadership skills. Each portion of the text is testament to his attention to detail, his desire to help men become good fathers, and his enduring commitment to building robust families that honour God.

This book is required reading for anyone who desires to know and live out the essentials of God's plan for fathers and fatherhood. It is in that spirit that I commend *Unmasking Manhood* to you. This book will redefine your concept of fatherhood, focus your vision, encourage your heart, and influence your leadership style both as a man and as a father.

Emmanuel Kojo Hopeson, PhD
Rev. Minister, Professional Counsellor LCPC-AC,
ADR and Conflict Expert
President and Founder
Centre for Peace and Reconciliation
www.cpr.org.gh / www.drhopeson.com
Accra, Ghana

Introduction

"No word makes me happier than the word "daddy" uttered by one of my children."

- **MICHAEL JOSEPHSON**

THE NATIONAL URBAN LEAGUE of the USA has this as their slogan: *"Don't make a baby if you can't be a father."* That is a loaded statement, full of insights. In principle, no man must attempt to impregnate a woman until he is well equipped and ready to become a father, even if he is not ready to be a husband. It is honourable for a man to accept, affirm and feel proud to claim responsibility over a child he has fathered. It is only good fathers who must be celebrated. Fatherhood is not the act of producing a child; it is a calling and a great responsibility! That is the reason why responsible fathers are respected and honoured. As Sigmund Freud puts it rightly:

"I cannot think of any need in childhood as strong as the need for a father's protection."

Yes, every born child needs the protection of a caring father. Sadly, our world of today seem to find faults with whatever men do and even when a father plays a major role in his children's life, many a times they are not celebrated. As the great evangelist Billy Graham puts it: "A good father is one of the most unsung, unpraised, unnoticed, and yet one of the most valuable assets in our society." But I believe that this notion is gradually changing. Today, a lot of fathers are very much actively involved in the training and mentoring of their own children. That is very positive!

I wrote this book to spearhead my ministry as *a change agent* in the lives of men and fathers. My passion is to crusade for responsible fathers and highlight of great deeds some fathers are doing in the lives of their children and those they mentor. I seek to encourage men and fathers to bond and to work together to raise a new generation of responsible children. I seek to launch programmes and seminars to help and encourage fathers. That is why at the end of each chapter this book, I have summarized the key principles discussed within that chapter, to assist fathers in meeting and discussing these principles. This will ultimately help to improve their fathering skills and practices.

GOD'S ORIGINAL PLAN FOR MEN IS TO RAISE CHILDREN

EVERY MAN IS CALLED TO BE A MENTOR. Fatherhood is the first and most important calling of any man - single, married, divorced, remarried or widowed, this is also in reference to men who are unable to father children biologically, but still have the opportunity to mentor. In my estimation, any man who lives into his old age and has not mentored or offered fathering to other men is a real failure in life. If a man lives to become successful in all areas of his life but fails to multiply himself in other men, he has failed big time. I call such a man a *masked man* and I will explain why later in the chapters of this book.

I believe strongly that fatherhood is a major calling of every man. I believe that *fathering* is a key responsibility and a calling. Any man who bears the title father is tasked with doing what God is doing: being our Father in heaven. That is a herculean task, to do on earth, what God in heaven does. That is why I am teaching in this book that, fathering is both a *calling* and an *art*.

I describe fatherhood as a *calling* because, God has already programmed it in the nature or genes of men to be able to be responsible, to lead and to guide their children and help them catch a vision for their future. All man carries in them a fatherhood potential or an innate ability to offer training and guidance to children, either children of their own or mentoring other children.

When he has been able to develop this God-given 'raw material' – or potential - in him, a father is able to: "*Train the child the way he should go and he will never depart from it when he grows old*" (Proverbs 22:6). Fathers are mandated with the responsibility in training their children well and not to provoke their children to wrath (Ephesians 6:4). Fathers should therefore be considerate and not to irritate their children by vexatious commands or appropriate unreasonable blames on them. A responsible father should give encouragement rather than constant criticisms to his children.

A great father is the one who has developed his skill in offering protection and counsel to his children. He guides his children. He shows his children kindness as well as teaches them how to remain tough during hard times. It is a godly father's divine responsibility to care for and guide his children.

A father's *duty* includes helping children to discover their purpose and know the plan of the Creator for their lives. Note also that, fatherhood is an art because it is an ability that must be developed into a skill. A father becomes a good father when he has himself received mentoring and has developed his knack of fathers.

We can therefore learn how to be a father, before we can do the work of a father. The work of being a father is what we are unmasking in this book. You need not have your own biological children to earn the title *father* or be addressed as a *father*.

As long as you are a male, you are born with the innate ability to father children. You are designed for fatherhood. Fatherhood is in your DNA. You will never be fulfilled in life until you have unmasked yourself and began to minister unto other men – younger men – and be a father to them. As long as you are a man, you must be a father to the fatherless. That is the key to being fulfilled in life and living a life of significance. The earlier you accept this truth, the better.

Fathering goes far beyond the act of impregnating a woman. That simple act can be carried out by any man. In fact, even male dogs can impregnate as many female dogs as possible – even including its own mother and sisters! It's pitiable to draw these comparisons but the stark reality is there are many men who act like such dogs; they go about sowing their wild oats and siring many children, leaving them to be raised by single mothers. 'It is a reality that damages real and potentially rewarding relationships between father and child, instead it perpetuates the culture of fatherlessness, and such a man has failed.'

FATHERHOOD IS A SERIOUS BUSINESS

FATHERHOOD IS A SERIOUS BUSINESS and it takes men who have properly gone through the process of being boys, matured and graduated into manhood to be fit for such a task. These men have gone through the nitty-gritty of manliness. They have made all the basic mistakes of manliness and have learned great lessons from them. They have had scars of life that now make them stars.

They know how to live a life and have embraced responsibility. They have learned how to be a man enough to woo a woman, date her, court her and marry her and bear children with her. They are able to take good care of their families. These are men who have successfully graduated into manhood and fatherhood. They have learnt the art of being a responsible man and have learnt what it takes for a man live with a woman, love her and bear kids with her and take good care of them and mentor his children. That is what I call: *Unmasking Fatherhood.*

In *Unmasking Fatherhood*, I seek to make clear the fact of life that, men are not born already made. **Boys are born, men are made, and fathers are given.** A boy must go through a process of mentoring to learn to be a good man. A good man goes through a process of maturity to become qualified to be a husband and a father. These take a process, and I call that process *unmasking*. BY THE PROCESS OF UNMASKING, a boy goes through a systematic training to initiate him unto manliness, long before he dreams of becoming a husband and a father. Thus, no boy should become a man without going through some kind of training to become a man. No man should get married until he has gone through a process or trainings and maturation steps. A married man should undergo some learning process before deciding to be a father. These are the processes I term as unmasking manhood and unmasking fatherhood.

Every man must learn to understand himself and accept the reality that we are designed differently to women, and that, women were fashioned in such a way that, they have what we do not have, and we have what they do not have.

In other words, women are designed with what it takes to meet the core needs of men, while men are designed with what it takes to meet the needs of women. That is why when God created the Eve for Adam; He revealed that she shall be the *helpmate* of the man. It is therefore a delusion for a woman to assume that she can do what a man was designed to do and vice versa.

The male and female were designed to *complement* each other, and not to *compete* with each other! An unmasked man and an unmasked father knows this truth and put it in practice in both the home and at the marketplace. Why? Because as an unmasked man, he understands his purpose and does not abuse it. He lives a purpose-driven life as a man and as a father.

Indeed, manhood is *a state of being* and fathering is a lifetime *ministry*. For example, only men who have developed their manliness can become responsible fathers. By manliness, I am referring to the process of developing one's masculinity and living according one's design as man. A man is different from a woman in both design and function, and these must be learnt through the process of unmasking.

Fathers have a critical role in shaping who and what their children would become in future. Fathers offer affection and affirmation to their children, especially their sons. Fathers give identity to their children. Fathers bless – or curse – their children, not only with words of mouth, but by the genetic information they transmit to their children at conception. *To a large extent, fathers can determine where their children will spend eternity.* This may come as a surprise, but the relationship and results of fathering has greater impacts than we appreciate.

FATHERHOOD IS NOT MEANT FOR BOYS!

FATHERHOOD IS NOT A TITLE. Fatherhood is a calling, a ministry and a lifetime responsibility. Until you acknowledge these truths, you will be in danger of abusing women and using sexual intercourse as a mere means of releasing stress and pressure. In this book, *Unmasking Fatherhood*, my primary purpose is to help open the eyes of my fellow men to know our purpose on earth and how we can deploy our purpose and maximize our potential as responsible, godly fathers and as successful fathers and mentors.

As men and as fathers, we are on earth to make impact on the next generation. We are not called just to father children. As men, we are messengers sent by God to team up with women to raise generations of godly people and to make the earth a better place to live.

As unmasked fathers, we are sent as God's agent to train children and prepare them to live purpose-driven lives on earth, and to prepare them for eternity. So a father never completes his ministry of fathering. As fathers, we are mandated to father our children at different stages of their lives – from infancy, children, adolescence and adulthood.

As kids, our children helplessly look up to us for affection and for accountability. As teens, our sons and daughters – in spite of their rebellion and stubbornness – look up to us for identity and for direction. *You have done a good job as a father, when your daughter confesses that she wants a husband who is like you or better. You have succeeded as a great father, when your son respects you and admires your work and wishes to do the same work you do one day, even if he chooses to pursue a different career!*

THIS BOOK WILL HELP YOU as a young man and as an adult. This book will help you as a woman and as a wife. How? You will discover what you did not know about men, and help you appreciate your husband more and be willing to help him achieve his fatherhood goals. It will also help heal your own *father wound* if you did not have a good relationship without your own father, as a growing child.

RICHARD AKITA
ACCRA, GHANA

CHAPTER 1

FATHERHOOD: MAN'S HIGHEST CALLING

"Of all the rocks upon which we build our lives, we are reminded...that family is the most important. And we are called to recognize and honor how critical every father is to that foundation. They are teachers and coaches. They are mentors and role models. They are examples of success and the men who constantly push us toward it."[1]

– PRESIDENT BARACK OBAMA

FATHERHOOD IS IN CRISIS! If you doubt it, check out each year's Fathers' Day. What do we see on Fathers' Day? Most often, it's a dry day for most men and fathers. Instead of being a happy day of celebration, many people - including many men – rather become emotional and do not celebrate *Fathers' Day*. Compared to *Mothers' Day*, fathers are far less celebrated; even responsible fathers tend to not celebrate their own fathers. It is for this reason that I want us to examine fatherhood in this chapter.

WHAT IS FATHERHOOD? Who is a father? What is God's Fatherhood and God's vision for fatherhood? Why is it that many fathers do not seek to bless their children, and instead fathers run around seeking to receive blessings of others? These

---

[1] © 2015 The New York Times Company

questions will be answered throughout this book, but in this first chapter, I want us to examine the root problem with our appreciation of fatherhood, and solutions to our unanswered fatherhood questions.

In our world of today, virtually every societal problem can be traced back to fatherhood. Our society is bereft with social injustice, upsurge of crimes, behavioural disorders, sexual perversions, juvenile delinquency, sexual molestations, and many more. Who is behind such abnormal acts? Men. Sexually immoral fathers, who do not respect or understand their enormous calling, who commit heinous acts of sexual violence including raping women, and at times, their own daughters. I read statistics carried out in USA by the *Girl Scouts Research Institute*. These were their findings:

- *90% of all women want to change at least one aspect of their appearance, and only 2 percent of women think they are beautiful.*
- *81% of 10 year olds are afraid of being fat.*
- *A girl is being bullied every 7 minutes.*
- *Every 15 seconds a woman is battered.*
- *50% of music videos portray women as sex objects, victims, or in a condescending way.*
- *1 of 4 college women has an eating disorder.*
- *1 out of 3 girls between the ages of 16-18, say sex is expected from them at their age if they are in a relationship.*

At a disproportionate rate, young girls often find themselves mistreated, misused, and under-valued by the male figures in their lives – including their fathers. Every daughter longs for a deep connectedness with her dad. Every girl needs guidance, boosting of self-esteem, honour and being celebrated as worthy, and a father must provide these. Of course, this goes for sons too, but sons also have a different set of needs.

You may be wondering why I have stated the need of a daughter for a deeper bond with her father. But the question is who makes a woman? Apart from God, who is her Creator. Here on earth, it is men, and the chief amongst the men in a young girl's life is her dad! Every girl needs her father's affirmation and admiration from an early stage. Every girl needs a godly father who is well-informed, secure and sound in his spirit, soul (*mind, emotions* and *will*) and in his body.

The fact is that men are appointed by God to make our children secure. God's highest calling for man is for him to be a husband or a father. How do I know this? God Himself is the Source of Fatherhood. God is the Chief Model of Fatherhood and all fatherhood matters begin with Him and ends with Him.

Any form of fathering style that does not go in line with what He has revealed in His Word, is abnormal and faulty. God has chosen to represent Himself as our heavenly Father. Jesus Christ affirmed this truth, when He taught us to pray, the first words we are instructed to use whilst praying is: "**Our Father Who art in heaven...**"

You can never talk appropriately about fatherhood without a reference to God, the Father. Until we relate to God as our Father, we would not have Him working effectively in our lives. We must acknowledge Him as our Father, first before He comes into our lives. We must have an active relationship with Him, through His Only Beloved Son, Jesus Christ, in order for us to enjoy His Sonship.

Without a good and continuous relationship with the heavenly Father, we will lack self-confidence, feel insecure, and unworthy of ourselves as men, because only God as our Father has the power to show us how to be good and caring fathers on earth. We need His acceptance, His affirmation and His direction to know how we can offer effective fathering to our own children or those who look up to us as fathers and mentors.

Without a good relationship and connection to the Fatherhood of God, none of us human fathers can have our gifts reinforced, and our source of love would be blocked, leaving us without a blueprint to follow. Thus, every father in earth needs to connect to the Father in heaven, and to worship Him *"in Spirit and in truth"* as Jesus told the woman of Samaria in John 4.

Until that woman caught the revelation of the Fatherhood of God and the Sonship of the Lord, she was bound by the negative social labels people put on her – as an immoral woman. When she saw God as the Father, she was liberated and her past life was replaced by a new life in Christ. Her broken self-esteem was restored as she enjoyed true fatherhood first time in her life! You can also enjoy the same today!

OUR RELATIONSHIP WITH GOD AS FATHER

Before we can successfully connect to and relate positively to God as our heavenly Father, we need earthly dads who are good models of fatherhood in our lives. God is the ultimate model of fatherhood to follow, but He works *through* earthly fathers. That is why we need fathers at all cost. Even if you do not have a biological father in your life, you need a positive male figure who will play this role. It is a must. Fatherhood is the highest calling of men, and it takes men who are fathers to help us imitate our heavenly Father.

The Bible declares God as our Father who is Almighty and Everlasting, our Refuge and Fortress and our Shepherd. He is strong, ever-present, and His love is everlasting. He is our Rock that holds us secure in Christ. He is our very Source of unconditional love. He is our emotional Anchor, our Provider, our Chief Mentor, our Nurturer and Director General. These are all great qualities of the Heavenly Father that every earthly dad should aspire to become.

The good news is this; He has not left us fatherless. God the Father has given our dads the opportunity to tap into God's Fatherhood. That is how children can feel loved and secure and see our true identity as unmasked men and as fathers. When the Spirit of God's Fatherhood engulfs a man, we are empowered to see, as Paul puts it, *Abba, Father.*

*"The Spirit you received does not make you slaves, so that you live in fear again; rather, the Spirit you received brought about **your adoption to sonship**. And*

by him we cry, *"**Abba, Father.**"The Spirit Himself testifies with our spirit that we are God's children."*

As fathers who have been fathered by the heavenly Father Himself, we must see the urgency of the need to step up our game and responsibility and treat our children like God treats us. As we are free to call God, *Abba, Father*, we must make room for our children to feel excited to call us dads! I encourage you as a fellow father to begin from today, to bless your children each day. Say words of blessing and words of exhortation onto your children. Affirm them. Let them feel appreciated. Correct them when they go wrong. Guide them. Above all, live by example for them to see.

Let your sons know that they are developing well from boyhood unto manhood. Help unmask the raw man inside them. Help unearth, develop and deploy their potential and maximize it. Help them renew their mind and retrain their minds to become responsible men and godly men. Teach them how to succeed in life. Mentor them.

Make a good effort to celebrate your father this year's **Father's Day**. If you are a dad like I am, let us take a cue from Jacob, and lay hands and bless our children. Let us slow down on chasing after blessings, and know that we carry in us the power to bless and to be a blessing. Let us serve instead of seeking to be served. Let us demonstrate love towards our children and they will love us back.

As dads, we must realize that, we have the highest calling on earth as fathers. Let us be a blessing to our children by teaching them about fatherhood and demonstrate by our words and actions, who a good father is supposed to be. If we do this very well, our children shall surely honour us!

Now the question is, how does a man, as a father, accomplish all that I have discussed in this opening chapter? When was the institution of fatherhood actually established here on earth? What was the original model and mandate of fatherhood as given by the Creator? These and many more, we shall examine and explore in the rest of the following chapters.

REFLECTIONS

- Can fatherhood be rescued?
- Why is fatherhood less celebrated?
- Can fathers determine the destiny of their children?
- What practical steps can a father follow to affirm their children?
- How do fathers deal with wayward children?

CHAPTER 2

FATHERHOOD BEGAN WITH ADAM

"Father! – to God Himself we cannot give a holier name!"

- **WILLIAM WORDSWORTH**

THE WORDS "FATHER" AND "FATHERS" occur about 1,650 times in the Holy Bible, and in the Book of Genesis close to 200 times. That is very significant to me, because Genesis is a book of beginnings, setting the sure foundation for the subsequent sixty-five books in the Bible. Thus, the repetitiveness of a particular word in Genesis has great significance – both theologically and historically.

Now, curiously, the word *"father"* is described as Strong's Concordance's #1 Hebrew word *Abba,* used especially in the New Testament. Abba simply means, *"Dad "*and I love that word *Abba.* Dads are number one and when that title is conferred on you by your children, it is very significant and a very serious matter. Why? Toddlers usually pronounce a variant of *"mother"* first, but *"father"* is often one of the first words spoken by a newly-born child in God's family!

It was a particular joy to many of us, a few moments after having trusted Christ, to bend the knees and begin to pray meaningfully for the first time, saying: *"Father…"* That we can address the Creator of the universe, the God of all the earth,

Jehovah, the Almighty, and call Him Father, is an awe-inspiring truth! The subject of the Fatherhood of God in the Bible is the most instructive. For example, notice Paul's carefully chosen words in his letter to the Ephesians:

"I bow my knees unto the Father of our Lord Jesus Christ, of Whom the whole family in heaven and earth is named."

- **EPHESIANS 3:14, 15**

WHAT DOES THIS MEAN? Among other things, Paul was teaching us that, as Father, *God is the original source of fatherhood!* The Heavenly Father is therefore the perfect pattern or role model or example for every father on earth. For Christian fathers in particular, we are mandated to take our cue from Him. He is our chief example. No human father is the best example. Indeed, the best of fathers even lack and cannot offer his children the best example of masculinity and fatherhood.

Only the Abba Father has it all! I have taken time to cite this key example so that you would not look up to man as a perfect example of fatherhood. Not even your biological father! Only the Heavenly Father should be your chief role model of masculinity and fatherhood. That is why the Lord Jesus Christ – a perfect example of Sonship – often referred to His Father in heaven, and attributed the source of all His success in ministry to Him!

Having established this solid foundation as key to unmasking manhood and fatherhood, let us now turn our attention to the first ever human father on earth. Adam. We will also look at several other fathers in the Book of Genesis and see how they measured up to the Fatherhood of God. Let us begin with Adam, our first earthly father.

ADAM: THE FIRST MAN AND FATHER

Note that, **Adam was the first man, first husband, and first father on earth**. This is a very significant truth to know whenever you want to touch on the subject of fatherhood. It is therefore right that we begin with him. He was created by God according to His own image and likeness. God put him in the Garden of Eden. God gave him a woman to marry. God Himself brought to him the first woman on earth, whom Adam named as Eve. She was brought to Adam by direct divine intervention. Her purpose was – and still is – to be the most suitable being or help mate for Adam.

This made Adam a very favoured man. We do not know how long Adam enjoyed fellowship with God in that Garden of Eden, but the quality of that fellowship also equip him with the ingredients necessary to become one of the best fathers this world has ever seen!

GOD'S PURPOSE FOR CREATING MAN

BEFORE THE CREATOR CREATED anything on earth, He already had a clear-cut purpose and plan for all creatures He had in mind. Going through the first chapter of the first Book of the Holy Scripture, it is crystal clear that God is the Creator of everything in the universe, both the visible and the invisible. After having created all things – both the living and the non-living – here on earth, He crowned it all on the sixth day, by creating Man.

In Genesis 1 God gives an overview of the entire creation history, including man and woman. Genesis 2 provides details relating to their actual creation. Our interest is in His human creation. What can we learn of God's original plan for mankind?

*"Then God said, "Let us make **man** in our image, in our likeness, and let **them** rule over the fish of the sea and the birds of the air, over the livestock, over all the earth, and over all the creatures that move along the ground."*

- **GENESIS 1:26, NIV**

The English word *"man"* used in the above is *adam* in Hebrew which translates as mankind or human being. It is used here as a common noun not the name of a man nor a reference to males only. This is true not only in this verse but in many others in the creation account. Note that it says "let **them** rule…"

*"So God created **man** (adam = mankind) in His own image, in the image of God He created him; male and female He created them."*

- **GENESIS 1:27, NKJV**

The Word proclaims mankind, both male and female, in the image and likeness of God. "Image" according to Strong's means *representative figure.* The man and woman were the beginning place for Him to reveal Himself - His image - on the earth.

*"Then God blessed **them,** and God said to **them**, "Be fruitful and multiply; fill the earth and subdue it; have dominion over the fish of the sea, over the birds of the air, and over every living creature that moves on the earth."*

- **GENESIS 1:28, NKJV**

God is speaking to both when He commands them to multiply, subdue and have dominion. Dominion is over the creatures, not each other. It is also important to note that subdue, *kabash* in Hebrew, indicates that there is something in the earth that is hostile and must be conquered. Now, this creation, and all of it, was **very good**:

"And God saw all that He had made, and it was very good..."

- **GENESIS 1:31, NKJV**

*"The Lord God **formed the man** from the dust of the ground and breathed into his nostrils the breath of life and **the man** became a living being."*

- **GENESIS 2:7, NIV**

In this case the scripture no longer says just "man" but specifies "the man" referring to Adam, a particular man. The man, Adam, was formed first from the dust of the ground. The Hebrew word for *formed* is a different word from that for created. It speaks of development rather than original creation. "Adam and Eve were created simultaneously, but Adam was formed, elaborated, first."

*"And out of the ground the Lord God made every tree grow that is pleasant to the sight and good for food. The **tree of life** was also in the midst of the garden, and the tree of the knowledge of good and evil."*

- **GENESIS 2:9, NKJV**

Having formed Adam, God provides food, both physical and spiritual. Both will be necessary for mankind to become what God created them to be. The critical nature of this verse will be seen in Genesis 2:16-17.

"The Lord God took the man and put him in the Garden of Eden to cultivate it and keep it."

- **GENESIS 2:15, NASB**

The word *keeps* in the Hebrew, according to Strong's Concordance (8104), means *to hedge about*. That is to: guard, protect, attend to, indicating that there must have been something from which it needed to be protected. The same word is used in Genesis 3:24 when it refers to the Cherubim *keeping* the way to the tree of life.

*"And the Lord God **commanded** the man, saying, "Of every tree in the garden you **may freely eat**, but of the tree of the knowledge of good and evil, you shall not eat, for in the day that you eat of it you shall surely die."*

- **GENESIS 2:16-17, NKJV**

Did you notice that it says, "commanded the man?" Just what was it that was commanded? "May freely eat" sounds like giving permission but in the Hebrew context, there is a different connotation. "Neither the words *"may"* or *"freely"* indicate that God was leaving the 'if, when, or how much to eat' to Adam's own discretion. Adam, having free will, could choose not to eat of the provision God had made, but it would be in direct disobedience to the command."

Spiritual food was available from the tree of life, the very life of God, yet Adam did not choose to partake of this provision for "keeping" the garden. It is a principle of scripture that God offers provision before He gives us a job. The ability to "keep" the garden would come from partaking of the tree of life.

"The Lord God said, "It is not good for the man to be alone. I will make a **helper suitable** *for him...So the man gave names to all the livestock, the birds of the air and all the beasts of the field. But for Adam no suitable helper was found."*

- **GENESIS 2:18,20, NIV**

God once called creation *"very good"* and now he says "not good." How did the "very good" pronouncement become "not good?" Jacob Behman, the great German philosopher, said: "There must have been something of the nature of a stumble; if not an actual fall in Adam while yet alone in Eden...Eve was formed to help Adam to recover himself and to establish himself in Paradise, and in the favour, fellowship and service of his Maker."

This interpretation is supported by the definition of the word *"alone"*, which means something like **"alone in his separation."** If God had meant just that one person alone was not a desirable thing, then the Hebrew expression for *"one alone"*, as found in Isaiah 51:2, would seem more appropriate.

A second interpretation of the meaning of "not good for man to be alone" is that God knew Adam needed a mate, but Adam needed to see his need. By the time he finished naming the animals, it would be clear that he had no counterpart. Regardless of the state of Adam, we need to know what a **helper suitable** or as the KJV says, a help mate, is.

The word helper in Hebrew is **ezer,** and the word suitable in Hebrew is **kenego.** *Ezer* is used of woman two times, and of God helping his people fifteen times, and one time of God providing help through David. It also is used three times for military power.

In all the latter three categories the one helping is equal to or superior to the one being helped. Why would the first one be any different? *Kenegdo* means corresponding to or counterpart to, equal to or matching. This indicates complimenting or completing, an equal and perfect counterpart. The idea of **help mate** meaning an assistant created for man's comfort, pleasure and use.

"So the Lord God caused the man to fall into a deep sleep; and while he was sleeping, he took one of the man's ribs and closed up the place with flesh. Then

the Lord God made a woman from the rib he had taken out of the man, and he brought her to the man."

- **GENESIS 2:21-22, NIV**

The Creator formed the woman from material taken from the side of the man. The word used in Hebrew is *tslea*, which many translate as *rib*. But actually, when the word *tslea* is used, it is translated as: *side, corner, chamber* or *flesh*. As the Church came from the side of Christ, the Lord God took woman from the side of man. This is a beautiful typology. Eve was formed from Adam's substance and both were of human substance, yet formed differently. She was *the finishing touch* and completion of God's creation of mankind.

"The man said, "This is now bone of my bones and flesh of my flesh; she shall be called 'woman,' for she was taken out of man."

- **GENESIS 2:23, NIV**

The word *woman* in Hebrew is the feminine form of man. Indeed, in Hebrew, *ish* is used for man, and *ishshah* is used for woman. Adam called her woman recognizing in her the female version of himself - a human being - his perfect counterpart.

"For this cause a man shall leave his father and his mother and shall cleave to his wife; and they shall become one flesh and the man and his wife were both naked and not ashamed."

- **GENESIS 2:24,25, NASB**

GOD'S ORIGINAL PLAN FOR MARRIAGE

Marriage must be given top priority among human relationships. In her book, *Fashioned for Intimacy*, Jane Hansen wrote, "The union between the man and woman was to be inseparable; it was not to be divided." That is intimacy. In the fullest sense of the word, intimacy is far beyond what we often think of as the one flesh relationship, the sexual union. Sexual intimacy was given to be the seal, the celebration of a much greater and deeper intimacy, which was intended to follow - that of *heart, soul* and *spirit*. This kind of relationship would reflect, not only union with one another, but also with God.

IN EPHESIANS 5:25-32, Apostle Paul reveals that the relationship described here shows forth that of Christ and His Church. Man and Woman in unity with each other, and their Creator together showing forth the image of God! So fatherhood represents God's very nature as a spiritual Being, and in His magnanimity, the heavenly Father created the Man 'in His own image' so that Man would represent Him physically here on earth.

ADAM AS THE FIRST MALE-MAN GOD CREATED is mandated to show forth, God's great fatherhood on earth and serve as a great and a good father to his sons and daughters, even as God is the greatest and best Father of all of us. This makes human fatherhood a great work and a sacred responsibility. It is so great to be called a father, but to maintain that greatness requires that fathers be responsible and play our roles as great men and use our masculinity to help women fulfil their femininity to the glory of God! That is what I call authentic fatherhood and Adam was the first man ever to have tasted what it is to be a father.

THE FIRST AND THE LAST ADAM

THE NAME ADAM is mentioned about thirty times in the Bible. Eighteen of those references are in Genesis chapters 2 to 5. Sadly, anything about him after that - apart from chronological lists - has to do with his fall. Job 31:33 closes the Old Testament record on Adam, referring to his transgression and iniquity. Apostle Paul also did refer to Adam in the New Testament in line with his fall from grace to grass, and how God the Father sent His dear Son Jesus Christ to come as the Last Adam to redeem us and restore us to His Fatherhood:

"Therefore, just as sin came into the world through one man, and death through sin, and so death spread to all men because all sinned - for sin indeed was in the world before the law was given, but sin is not counted where there is no law. Yet death reigned from Adam to Moses, even over those whose sinning was not like the transgression of Adam, who was a type of the one who was to come. But the free gift is not like the trespass. For if many died through one man's trespass, much more have the grace of God and the free gift by the grace of that one man Jesus Christ abounded for many."

- **ROMANS 5:12-15**

THE NAME EVE appears four times in the Bible. It is one of three names that she had. Adam first called her *Woman* (Genesis 2:23), when he looked at her in relation to himself. He called her Eve (Genesis 3:20) when he considered her motherhood.

Finally, God called them both Adam (Genesis 5:2), linking them together but, sadly, as a fallen couple.

ADAM AND HIS FAITHLESSNESS

You have noticed that in that great chapter of the Bible, Hebrews 11, the name Adam is conspicuously missed out? Even though Adam was saved in the end, he is remembered more because of his fall than because his faith. What a sad record for a father!

Hebrews 11 is called the Bible's hall of fame and reading, you will find many men who were testified about in that great book. Dad after dad, story after story, God gives testimony of how great men and women of early Bible times were able to live for God because of their unswerving faith. You can read about Abraham, Noah, Abel and many others but strangely, Adam is not mentioned. Adam should have been included too, but he fell and failed all mankind! Why did the first human father fail?

Satan had fallen and was thrown out of heaven long before God created the Garden and put Adam in. He therefore had his eye on Eden's couple, as he does on families today! Eventually Eve was deceived and Adam disobeyed God. Adam tried to justify his fall by blaming his wife, Eve, and even the circumstances God had brought him into (Genesis 3:12), but God held Adam accountable for what happened (Romans 5:12).

ADAM'S FATHERHOOD started off banished from Eden and far from the place of fellowship and favour that God had intended for his posterity. That is a great lesson to us as today's fathers. Dear dads, whatever we do, let us be careful not to surrender the father's blessing that God has given us for our children. Adam failed God and in turn failed his children too. His first son Cain was eternally ruined by his father's fall, and the Flood swept all his descendants away, leaving no trace of Cain's heritage on earth – and this can happen to you as a father, if you disobey God and fail to raise your children well.

Consequence of Adam's disobedience led to his second son Abel dying prematurely a violent death. Even though it seems like Adam planted seeds of devotion and worship to God in Abel, he was slain by his wicked brother Cain. God replaced Abel with Seth, yet, Seth's children suffer from the evil consequences of the fall even to this day.

Apostle Paul referred to the Lord Jesus as "the last Adam" in I Corinthians 15:45, and not as "the second Adam." Why? Because Jesus Christ is God's ultimate final solution to our sin problem. That means, in Christ, there will not be another fall. We suffer from the first Adam's fall, but as believers we enjoy the last Adam's forgiveness and restoration to God's Fatherhood!

THE LESSON IS CLEAR: As dads, our spiritual downfall will not only affect ourselves and those around us today, but may well have drastic, hurtful, and lasting consequences on future generations! Sons and daughters who grow up under the stigma, shame, and sorrow of a father who fell from God will face many difficult circumstances in life. You probably know someone today who is struggling in life because of the iniquity of his father. That is why again, Apostle Paul counsel exhorts the Corinthians – and us - that:

"Let him that thinketh he standeth, take heed lest he fall."

- **I CORINTHIANS 10:12**

REFLECTIONS

- What is the role of a father in his fatherhood responsibilities?
- Why was Adam's name missing from the list of heroes in Hebrews 11?
- Can our action cause a ripple effect of blessings or curses?
- Why was the last Adam needed?
- Did Adam lack stewardship? If yes, did that lead to The Fall?

CHAPTER 3

FATHER ABRAHAM'S MODEL OF FATHERING

"For I know him, that he will command his children and his household after him, and they shall keep the way of the LORD, to do justice and judgment; that the LORD may bring upon Abraham that which he hath spoken of him."

- GENESIS 18:19, KJV

NEXT TO ADAM, the next most significant father figure in the Old Testament is Abraham. The patriarch Abraham is the father of three major religions on earth, namely: Judaism, Christianity, and Islam. Is that not amazing? How did he earn the awesome title *"father"*? Is it because he was a friend of God or that father of faith? Well, these may be part of the reason, but as far as I am concerned, Abraham earned these titles as a result of his *fathering style*.

Abraham was very much involved in the raising, training and upbringing of all that were in his household. He fathered all those in his household. Even long before he fathered children of his own. He effectively trained men and women in his household and guided their faith in God. No wonder God Himself made this testimony about Abraham:

"For I know him, that he will command his children and his household after him, and they shall keep the way of the LORD, to do justice and judgment; that the LORD may bring upon Abraham that which he hath spoken of him."

- **GENESIS 18:19, KJV**

This was a very significant part of Abraham's character. He did only pray with his family but he taught them as a man of knowledge. He went further to command them as a man in authority. He was indeed a father, a prophet, a king, as well as priest, in his own house. He did not only take care of his biological children, but of his entire household. He discipled his servants on the things of God. That sets a good example that, masters of families should instruct, and inspect the manners of all under their roof.

That is one of the most important roles of godly fathers: we are mandated to offer direction and instruction concerning God's Word in our homes and of those that were under his charge. Abraham's method of fatherhood so pleased God that God Himself undertook Abraham's education in order to address and to overcome the social human obstacles to righteous and reverent living.

Obstacles here are amply described in the pre-Abrahamic stories of Genesis. Now, long after the era of Noah, no man stood out as a worshipper of God in the Bible, until the name Abram appeared in Genesis 12. Abram became the new man, and later, as Abraham, became the founder of a new nation steeped in God's new way, which this nation was to carry as a light unto all the nations of the world. He became the faith of the Hebrews and the only reference of God's fatherhood during the early stage of the life of the Israelites. He had an everlasting covenant with God.

He brought a new way of living according to God's standards, in the world that was purely pagan and had no covenant relationship with Jehovah God. The new way Abraham brought entailed a rightful conduct toward and rightful relations with members of one's household, members of one's tribe, as well as strangers and members of other nations, and ultimately with God.

Abraham's education in matters of the home leadership is one of the best models of fatherhood. Educating the father of his people means, in the first instance, educating him to be a proper husband and father; for the perpetuation of God's new way will depend not on an unexpected succession of naturally virtuous men and women but on the proper rearing of the young in every generation to the task of transmitting their moral and spiritual heritage.

ABRAHAM'S EDUCATION IN FATHERHOOD

Abraham was presented with Sarah's education in motherhood. Central to this account would be the wondrous birth of Isaac, after eighty-nine years of infertility, which leaves no doubt that children are a gift, not a maternal product and possession! The pre-Abrahamic chapters of Genesis tell one crucial story that explores the uninstructed or natural ways of fathers and sons and the vexing difficulties which confounded their relationship: the story of Noah and his sons (Genesis 9:18-27).

Noah, after the flood, turned to the grape and was laid low by drink. Without his clothes on and laying prostrate in his tent in a drunken stupor, Noah laid there stripped of all respectability. Now, his disrespectful son, Ham, viewed his father in disgrace and ran to tell his brothers about his father's shame.

Noah as father was reduced to a mere helpless man, and that one act of indiscretion, he had abandoned his father-authority, and laid aside his roles as a mentor, as a guide, as teacher of the laws of God. The danger of such a reversion and shameful deed lurks in every household, both from the side of notorious fathers and from the side of irreverent sons.

THE INIQUITIES OF THE FATHERS are often visited upon the sons. Noah, awakening to discover what Ham had done, cursed Canaan the son of Ham. That was strange, he was driving a wedge between Ham and his own son! Ham later became the father of peoples and nations, including the Canaanites and the Egyptians, whose abominable sexual practices and, whose family life became the very opposite to that of the Jewish laws of purity. That is how powerful a father's curse can be. Son, may you never provoke your father to release a word of curse against your destiny!

In contrast, Shem, the son who piously covers his father's nakedness without even looking upon it, became the father of the line that leads to Abraham. Shem appears to have discerned the authoritative relationship between a father and son. Fathers and sons will both need instruction in how to promote family holiness and how to secure the work of the perpetuation of the lineage.

ABRAHAM'S PATERNAL BEGINNINGS

ABRAHAM HAD AN UNUSUAL FATHER: **Terah.** He had children very late. More importantly, he was a radical man who left behind the land and presumably also the ways of his fathers in search of something new. A severed link in his own cultural chain. Terah sets the example for Abraham's own radical living.

There is also something significant in the name Terah gave his first-born son: **Abram,** which means *"lofty or exalted father,"* or perhaps *"the father is exalted."* in either case, there is an expression of *paternal pride* at his birth. One of his three sons (Haran) died in his young manhood. His second son, Nahor, refused to follow his father on his journey toward Canaan, and the third, Abram, left him behind in Haran, where he lived alone for sixty years and died without heirs to bury him.

Though he stems from Noah's son Shem, and though he himself was more attached to his father than was his brother Nahor, Abram's immediate paternal ancestry was a challenge. Abram's condition as a homeless, godless, childless son of a radical man made him a natural candidate to respond to God's promise of land, seed, rule, and fame. But, for the same reasons, he was not well-educated in the art of successful fatherhood.

When God called Abram out of his father's house, Abram was clearly enticed by the promise of greatness and prosperity. The content of the prophetic promise was clearly political, and its scope was global: Abram will become the blessed founder of a great nation and will acquire a great name, and all the families of the earth will be blessed because of him. Abram was seventy-five years of age, he obeyed God and set off immediately, "*as the Lord had spoken unto him...and Lot went with him*" (Genesis 12:4).

The promise of founding a great nation might have seemed odd to a childless man, and so Abram maximized his prospects by taking not only his barren wife Sarai, but also his nephew Lot, the son of his deceased brother Haran, whom Abram adopted. When Abram arrived in Canaan, he found it occupied. God appeared and informed him, "*Unto thy seed will I give this land.*" God hinted that Abram would have seed, but the focus is on the land, the Promised Land. Abram was not yet thinking in a fatherly way then. But Circumstances changed.

After an episode in Egypt, Abram and Lot came to a parting of the ways, "*for their substance was great so that they could not dwell together. And there was strife between the herdsmen of Abram's cattle and the herdsmen of Lot's cattle*" (Genesis 13:6-7). Now grown wealthy and wishing to avoid trouble more than he wished to preserve his family intact: "*Let there be no strife, I pray thee, between me and thee...for we are brethren*" (Genesis 13:8). Abram offered Lot the first and finest choice of land.

Attracted by civilization, Lot chose the fertile plain of the Jordan, eventually settling in Sodom and Gomorrah, and the men "*separated themselves the one from the other*" (Genesis 13:11). But in the immediate sequel, Abram no doubt felt a sense of loss, and needed consolation, so God as his Father, intervened:

"*And the Lord said unto Abram **after that Lot was separated** from him: "**Lift up now thine eyes,** and **look** from the place where thou art, **northward and southward and eastward and westward,** for all the land which thou seest, to thee **I will give it, and to thy seed forever.** And I will make thy seed as the dust of the earth: so that if a man can number the dust of the earth, then shall thy seed also be numbered. Arise, walk through the land in the length and breadth of it; for unto thee I will give it.*"

- **GENESIS 13:14-17**

Compensating Abram for the recent loss of the more favourable land, God stressed in beginning and ending how the lost land and more would eventually be Abram's possession. But in the midst of it, addressing Abram's loss of his probable heir, God spoke explicitly and graphically about Abram's own unborn son. God tried to put Abram in a frame of mind that would make him gain insight of his forthcoming paternity. But Abram remained attuned to matters that were more political, and he still had not reconciled himself to the loss of Lot.

Now, Lot was indirectly the cause of the next episode, which, for the first time, would lead Abram to powerfully demonstrate his inclination to fatherhood. The kings of Babylon invaded Canaan to suppress a rebellion against their rule. The Canaanite kings are defeated, Sodom among the other cities was sacked, and Lot was taken captive. Abram, who initially had discreetly sat out the war, now, upon learning that his nephew was taken captive, led forth his band of trained 318 men army into battle and won a mighty victory!

They smote the enemy, pursuing them past Damascus, and brought back all the goods, all the people, and his kinsman Lot, who promptly returned to Sodom! Refusing the spoils of war, Abram attempted to return to his previous life but, he could not. His brush with death in battle, his fear of reprisals, and perhaps, too, the definiteness of Lot's separation weighed on his mind. God is, as usual, responsive and spoke to Abram in a vision, assuring him:

"Fear not, Abram, I am thy shield, thy reward shall be exceedingly(?) great."

- GENESIS 15:1

Abram now, for the first time was weighed down with a concern for his childlessness, a concern which his encounter with death had now made acute. Abram, who had met all of God's previous interventions with silence, now opened up and addressed the Almighty God for the first time, and with sorrow and with passion. As he cried on God, God now sought to give reassurance on the subject of inheritors:

"O Lord God, what wilt Thou give me, **seeing I shall die childless**, and the one in charge of my house is Eliezer of Damascus?...**Behold, to me Thou hast given no seed,** and, lo, my steward will be my heir."

- **GENESIS 15:2-3**

"This man shall not be thine heir; but he that shall spring forth from thine own loins shall be thine heir." And He brought him forth abroad, and said: "Look now towards heaven, and count the stars, if thou be able to count them"; and He said unto him: "So shall thy seed be."

- **GENESIS 15:4-5**

With a more specific promise about his own offspring, and a loftier image to convey that they were innumerable, God for the time being calmed Abram's fears and eased his anxiety and fears. Abram impatiently demanded proof that he would indeed inherit the Promised Land. God agreed and enacted an awe-inspiring covenant.

As the pieces of the slain sacrifice laid on the ground, an eerie darkness engulfed Abram. God then spoke, but more of the future than present. I can imagine how Abram felt. The prophecy: he and his seed would inherit the land, but only after they had suffered four hundred years of slavery as strangers in a strange land! God concluded with remarks about Abram's own destiny:

"But thou shalt go to thy fathers in peace; thou shalt be buried in a good old age. And in the fourth generation they shall come back hither..."

- **GENESIS 15:15-16**

Abram now, more than ever, longed for a son. It was in this frame of mind that he received and eagerly accepted Sarai's offer to try to have a child of his own by Hagar the Egyptian. God neither interfered with nor approved the surrogate arrangement, and Abram got the son he wanted in Ishmael. At age eighty- six and a father at last! Now, what we can learn from this is that: **fatherhood is more than merely giving birth**, just as God's supernatural way is more than the way of nature.

Now that Abram has a son. As Ishmael approached young manhood (age thirteen), God, looking to the future, proposed a new covenant, giving Abram a new charge: *"**Walk before me and be thou whole-hearted** and I will make My covenant between thee and Me, and will **multiply thee exceedingly**"* (Genesis 17:1-2). The new covenant was announced in an unambiguous relation to the theme of procreation and perpetuation.

God's part of the covenant was very generous and full: He identified Himself to Abram (for the first time) as *"God Almighty,"* He promised Abram and fittingly renamed him *"Abraham,"* which means, *"father of multitudes."* God promised that He would make Abraham exceedingly fruitful, and the father of nations and the progenitor of kings. He promised that He would make an everlasting covenant with the seed of Abraham to be their God; He would give unto them the land of Canaan as an everlasting possession.

As for Abraham (and his seed), the obligation was simple: keeping the covenant simply means *remembering* it. That is, marking its token or sign in the flesh of every male throughout the generations, by the act of circumcision. Why should this covenant between God and Man be marked by circumcision?

Unlike the rainbow, the natural sign of God's earlier covenant with Noah and all life after the Flood, circumcision was an unnatural sign. It was the *memorial* of an agreement that deemed it necessary. It was to be made by man, marked by the organ of generation. Circumcision emphasizes the natural and the generative, sanctifying the circumcised person in the process.

The obligation of circumcision calls parents to the parental task. Performed soon after birth, it circumcises their pride, reminding them that children are a gift, for which they are not themselves creatively responsible. More importantly, they are called from the beginning to assume the obligations of transmission. They are compelled to remember, beginning with Abraham who was called and who sought to walk before God and to be whole-hearted.

They are reminded that bearing the child is the easy part, that *rearing him well* is the real vocation. They are summoned to continue the chain by rearing their children looking up to the divine, by initiating them into God's chosen ways. They are made aware of the consequences for their children - now and hereafter - of their failure to hearken to the call:

"And the uncircumcised male...that soul shall be cut off from his people: he hath broken My covenant."

- **GENESIS 17:14**

WITH CIRCUMCISION, the child, and all his potential future generations, are symbolically offered *by covenant* to the way of God. Question is, why was the rite applicable only to the male children? Because males especially need extra stimulus to undertake the parental role, men need to be acculturated to the work of transmission. Virility and sexual potency are, from the Biblical point of view, *much less* important than decency, righteousness, and holiness.

BY CIRCUMSICION, the father is recalled to this teaching, and *symbolically* remakes his son's masculinity for generations to come. When he comes of age, the son will also come to understand the meaning of the mark of his fathers and their covenant with God. In all probability, it will decisively affect how the circumcised son to use his sexual powers and how he looks on the regenerative and nurturing powers of woman.

As Abraham prepared to execute the covenant, he first circumcised himself (and he was at age ninety-nine). He then circumcised Ishmael and all the males in his household. God then announced that Sarah would bear him a son, and name him Isaac. This was to happen within one year. Now, Isaac, son of Sarah - not Ishmael, son of Hagar – was to be Abraham's *true heir* within this new covenant.

Abraham resisted the suggestion, partly out of disbelief, and partly out of his attachment to his first-born. Abraham at this stage had been giving Ishmael basic training in all knowledge of God that a father must pass on to his son. But he did not know he was just practicing to become the father of Isaac! Soon Isaac was born, and Abraham obediently circumcised his son Isaac. Many years later, on Mount Moriah, he fully understood what it truly meant.

FATHER OR FOUNDER: A PAINFUL LESSON

To this point we have been emphasizing how Abraham was being educated to understand that founding a great nation and gaining a great name requires a concern for progeny and transmission of character in one's son. This required rearing one's sons in full memory of God's kindness and His care as the Father. Again, Abraham was here still in the midst of an advanced education about the meaning of the role of his wife, without whom, he could not enter into proper fatherhood.

This sobering instruction greatly altered Abraham's view of the world, including his understanding of fatherhood. He began to see that proper fatherhood must be grounded not on the *natural love* of your own, but on the *acquired love* of what is right and what is good. This brings us back to the famous conversation between God and Abraham, concerning the fate of Sodom and Gomorrah. God arranged the encounter, testifying that: "seeing that Abraham shall surely become a *great and mighty nation*, and all the *nations shall be blessed in him*," and revealed for the first time His true interest in Abraham:

"For I have known him, to the end that **he may command his children and his household after him**, *that they may keep the ways of the Lord,* **to do righteousness and justice:** *to the end that the Lord may bring upon Abraham that which He hath spoken of him."*

- **GENESIS 18:17-19**

Abraham, the founder of a great nation, must do righteousness and justice, and command his children after him to do likewise, for only in this way could Abraham bring the Lord's righteous ways to the entire world, and thus be a blessing to all the nations of the earth. Although he had shown himself to be personally just, Abraham, because he was to be a *political* founder, needed also some instruction in political justice, that is, in justice regarding whole communities or cities or nations.

THE MEANING OF FATHERHOOD

Abraham, called by God to be the father of a new nation that would carry God's righteous ways to the rest of the world, was educated by God Himself in the proper roles of father and founder, and proved his readiness in his final test. After this, he had but a few remaining tasks to perform in order to complete his work as *father-founder*, after which he could quietly leave the scene.

Abraham purchased the cave at Machpelah as a burial place for Sarah, a deed simultaneously of ancestral and political significance; done not least for Isaac's and his descendants' sake. Abraham himself would also be buried here, as would Isaac and Rebekah, Jacob and Leah. The ground was consecrated as a memorial, helping to keep alive in memory the deeds of the founding mothers and fathers.

Ownership of this small plot of earth would be the Children of Israel's sole *legal claim* in the Promised Land during their four hundred years of exile in Egypt. Not agriculture but burial was the first title to land. The Holy Land is holy *first* because it was the land where the fathers of faith died!

Abraham next completed the work of perpetuation by arranging an appropriate marriage for Isaac. No father worth his salt could be indifferent to who it is his children marry. In Rebekah, he found more than any father of sons could ask for: a woman of worth whom, even more than her husband, would be responsible for safe-guarding the new way into the third generation.

AT AGE 175, HIS WORK WAS COMPLETE. Abraham *"expired, and died in a good old age, an old man, and full of years; and was gathered to his people. And Isaac and Ishmael his sons buried him in the cave of Machpelah...There was Abraham buried, and Sarah his wife. And it came to pass after the death of Abraham, that God blessed Isaac his son"* (Genesis 25:8-11).

ABRAHAM IS THE MODEL FATHER, both of his family and of his people, and to all of us! Even in his willingness to sacrifice his son, because he revered God, the Source of life and all divine covenants and blessing. A *true* father will devote his son to, and will self-consciously and knowingly initiate him into only the righteous and godly ways. He would understand that, like Abraham, only a father who feels awe before the true source can deserve the filial awe and reverence of his sons.

By showing his willingness to sacrifice what was his for what was right and good, he also puts his son on the proper road for his own adulthood: the true test of the good father. He would *not* finally love his son solely because he is *his own*, but would love only that in *his* son which is good and which is open to the good, including his son's own capacity for awe before the divine. In this sense, he was ever willing to part with his son as his son, recognizing him. As was Isaac, and as are indeed all children, as a gift and a blessing from God!

Just as Abraham as true father learned the limits on the love of one's own, so Abraham as the true founder learned the limits of politics and of the founder's pride. All founders, like all nations, look up to something. A *true* founder knows from the start that there is something higher and Someone higher than founding and higher than politics, in the light of which one should found or pioneer and father any project on earth. Righteous politics requires not only a desire for greatness, but a willingness to subordinate that desire to the very Source of righteousness.

FINALLY, the true founder knows and accepts the fact that his innocent sons would suffer for the sake of the righteous community and that their sacrifice is no proof that they are not properly loved as sons. The true founder, like the true father, shows his love for his followers when he teaches them, often by example, that one's life is not worth living if there is nothing worth dying for! What a great and eye-opening lesson for fathers!

FATHERHOOD IS NOT FATHERHOOD WITHOUT SONSHIP

BEFORE I CONCLUDE, let me talk a bit on Isaac. Indeed, aside the definition of fatherhood from Abraham's point of view, I must stress here that, *fatherhood is not fatherhood without sonship*. Can you imagine what Isaac might have felt, and learned, during his ordeal on Mount Moriah? On the surface, it looked that what Abraham was about to do was tragic and self-defeating: destroying the very evidence that he was indeed, the father of many nations. At age 130 and no other child apart from Isaac, yet he was about to destroy the life of his only and most beloved son.

Now here is the scene on the mountain. The old man Abraham, bound his 30-year-old son, Isaac. Amazingly, Isaac did not resist being bound. He was obedient, *"even as unto death."* Isaac did not struggle. Isaac did not even cry out. Isaac, it seemed, was complicit in his own sacrifice. That a very costly act by Abraham and a very compliant attitude by a son who dared not disobey his father. Pause and think about it. How many fathers will be bold enough to attempt this, and how many sons will be so obedient to the level Isaac was?

In fact, a closer look at the story of Abraham after this pivotal event seems to show that Isaac's relation to his father broke down as a result of the trauma he underwent. For example, going up the mountain, the writer stressed twice: "*they went* **both of them together**," but at the end of the story, the writer reported clearly that, "Abraham *returned unto his youths, and* **they** *rose up and* **went together** *to Beer-Sheba; and* **Abraham** *dwelt at Beer-Sheba*" (Genesis 22:19).

This indicates that Isaac did accompany his father down the mountain. However, if this hypothesis is true, then it would suggest that Abraham dwelt alone without Isaac, who is traumatized from the incident. In fact, after that event, we read nothing about Isaac and Abraham being together again until Isaac and Ishmael went together to bury Abraham.

Isaac was grieved by the death of his mother, Sarah, but same was not said about the death of his beloved father. If this is true, then I caution all fathers to be circumspect when it comes to taking unilateral action concerning the life of our grown children, especially our sons!

As I studied carefully and soberly the story of the latter part of Abraham, I concluded that, the "trauma" that Isaac experienced at the hands of his own father might explain why Isaac himself subsequently demonstrated gross shortcomings as a father of his own sons, Esau and Jacob. Just as Abraham with Ishmael and Isaac, Isaac also showed a biased preference for his son Esau, who is described in the Bible as *"strong, ruddy, earthy, present-cantered hunter."*

ISAAC LOVED ESAU, simply because, but not limited to, he loved to eat venison (red meat). Isaac seemed apparently indifferent to the paternal work of passing on legacy to the next generation. Everything pointed to the fact that Isaac neither understood nor approved of what his father did or stood for. Sadly, that is the shortcoming of many of us sons!

Many of us discover very late in our lives, that our parents get smarter as we get older. This is especially if we are blessed by God with children of our own to nurture, train, raise and mentor. Soon the reality dawns on us that our parents were really right when they said to us: *"You just you wait until you have children of your own, and then you'll see!"* It's amazing how we all as kids and youth, fail to learn to live under our parents' rule.

I suggest therefore that, as we mature into young adults, we must separate ourselves from our parents and establish a new life of our own – of course, without neglecting them. When we do that, we learn the hard way, and after that, we are able to return, step up to take their place as they grow older.

This, I believe, happened to Isaac, even though late in his life. This happened when Isaac discovered that he had been fooled by his younger son, Jacob, into giving him the blessing he had intended for Esau. This revelation suddenly brought Isaac to his senses. It's remarkable to note that, Isaac was not angry, but rather he was awe-struck:

"And Isaac trembled with an exceedingly great trembling."

- **GENESIS 27:33**

I am sure he sensed that the Abrahamic blessing had been given through him to the rightful son, under divine influence, far beyond his control. He had declared - prophetically - without knowing, when he sent Esau out at the start of this episode, he would eat but *his soul* would bless (Genesis 27:4) and so it happened. Despite himself, with the power of God residing in him, gave the blessing to the son for whom it was divinely directed. Note that in doing so he symbolically sacrificed his favourite son Esau! No wonder he trembled, perhaps saying:

"O my God! Is this what my father Abraham suffered, understood and felt on Mount Moriah?"

In the immediate outcome, Isaac on his own initiative called, blessed, and commanded Jacob not to take a Canaanite wife, but to find one at the ancestral home of his mother, Rebekah. Now here the last words and the last deed of Isaac recorded in the Bible. Isaac fully and freely bestowed on Jacob, the Abrahamic blessing: the proper blessing of the sons, which is covenant-based. Here were his words:

"And God Almighty will bless thee, and make thee fruitful, and multiply thee, that thou mayest be an assembly of peoples; And give thee the blessing of Abraham, to thee, and to thy seed with thee; that thou mayest possess the land of thy sojournings, which God gave unto Abraham."

- **GENESIS 28:3-4**

By these words, Isaac stepped into the prophetic role of fathers. At long last, he fulfilled his mission as a patriarch, taking over the father's baton from his father Abraham. Leadership and fatherhood mantle was transferred from one generation unto the next one. Isaac stood between the legacy of Abraham and that of his own children, Esau and Jacob.

The last word we hear from Isaac's lips is the name of Abraham, his father! That is one of the greatest models of fatherhood we can find in the Bible. I recommend to 21st Century fathers, especially, fathers of the Judeo-Christian faith.

REFLECTIONS

- What lesson can be derived from Abraham's fatherhood style?
- What are the implications of generational blessings?

CHAPTER 4

FATHERS AND FATHERHOOD

"One father is more than a hundred Schoolmasters."

- **GEORGE HERBERT, 1640**

A FATHER IS THE MALE PARENT OF A CHILD. Besides the paternal bonds of a father to his children, the father may have a parental, legal and social relationship with the child that carries with it certain rights and obligations, although this varies between jurisdictions. An *adoptive father* is a male who has become the child's parent through the legal process of adoption. A *biological father* is the male genetic contributor to the creation of the baby, through sexual intercourse or sperm donation.

A biological father may have legal obligations to a child not raised by him, such as an obligation of monetary support. A *putative father* is a man whose biological relationship to a child is alleged but has not been established. A *stepfather* is a male who is the husband of a child's mother and they may form a family unit, but who generally does not have the legal rights and responsibilities of a parent in relation to the child.

The adjective "paternal" refers to a father and comparatively to "maternal" for a mother. The verb "*to father*" means to procreate or to sire a child, which also derives from the noun "*fathering*". Biological fathers determine the sex of their child through a sperm cell which either contains an X chromosome (female), or Y chromosome (male). Related terms of endearment are *dad* (*dada, daddy*), *papa/pappa, papasita*, (*pa, pap*) and *pop*. A male role model that children can look up to is sometimes referred to as a *father-figure.*[2]

THE FATHER OF FATHERHOOD

IN EPHESIANS 3:14-15, Apostle Paul prayed: "*For this reason I bow my knees before the Father [**patēr**], from whom every family [**patria**] in heaven and on earth is named.*" In Greek it is easy to appreciate Paul's *patēr/patria* play on words. John Stott chose to translate this phrase as "*the Father from whom all fatherhood is named.*" The ESV translation footnote makes a similar point. That is what I call, the fatherhood of God, and the origin of fatherhood. You know, God's Fatherhood is the archetype of human fatherhood. This point is made even more explicit in Hebrews 12:7-11, which reads (NKJV);

*"If you endure chastening, God deals with you as with sons; for what son is there whom a father does not chasten? But if you are without chastening, of which all have become partakers, then you are illegitimate and not sons. Furthermore, we have had human fathers who corrected us, and we paid them respect. Shall we not much more readily be in subjection **to the Father of spirits** and live? For they indeed for a few days chastened us as seemed best to them, but He for our profit, that we may be partakers of His holiness. Now no chastening seems to be joyful for the present, but painful; nevertheless, afterward*

---

[2] Reference: From *Wikipedia*, the free encyclopaedia

it yields the peaceable fruit of righteousness to those who have been trained by it."

So God is the "Father of spirits" and that by implication means fathers are spirits. Hebrews chapter 12 is the only location in the entire Bible where this phrase is used. But what does it actually mean? I would not boast of being a theologian, so I leave the deeper interpretation to the Bible scholars. In my personal capacity, this is how I explain this: **Fathers take after God's nature**. Fathers are heads and leaders at home. Fathers are protectors over their family.

Fathers are authority figures and all the household is to look up to fathers. It is the duty of the father of a home to lay the blueprint for the home. He is the lawmaker as well as the teacher and the mentor of his children. A father's role is to correct, discipline and love his children. A father moulds the character and self-esteem of his children. Even as Jesus Christ always looked up to His Father in heaven, our children look up to us, as fathers!

As fathers of today, we take our cues on fatherhood from the Father of Fatherhood, which is a great relief for any father today who was fathered by a sinful or absent father (which of course includes every one of us). The most obvious feature of the Father of Jesus Christ is His generosity. He is generous with His glory, with His tasks, with His protection, with His home, and with His joy. The Father gives. The Father gives His Son; the Father gives His Spirit; the Father gives Himself. That is what fathers are required to do for their children.

"'He who has My commandments and keeps them, it is he who loves Me. And he who loves Me will be loved by My Father, and I will love him and manifest Myself to him." Judas (not Iscariot) said to Him, "Lord, how is it that You will manifest Yourself to us, and not to the world?" Jesus answered and said to him, "If anyone loves Me, he will keep My word; and My Father will love him, and We will come to him and make Our home with him. He who does not love Me does not keep My words; and the word which you hear is not Mine but the Father who sent Me."'

- **JOHN 14:22–24, NKJV**

Learning this about the Father who is a Spirit should stir up our spirits deeply. He is seeking worshipers who will worship Him in Spirit and in truth. In short, who will become like He is. And what is He like? He is generous with everything. Is there anything He has that he has held back? And what should we — tangible fathers — be like? The question is terribly hard to answer, but not because it is difficult to understand. That is a good challenge for me as a father because it makes me ask: from all the words that my children could use to describe me, would they choose *generous*? The answer spurs my attention to my Heavenly Father, the generous Father of all fatherhood.

REFLECTIONS

- How do Fathers take after God's nature?
- Who is responsible for laying the foundation of their home?
- What are the implications when a father moulds the character and self-esteem of his children?

CHAPTER 5

THE PURPOSE OF FATHERHOOD

"Purpose is inherent in everything that has been created."

- **DR. MYLES MUNROE**

THERE ARE PRINCIPLES that regulate everything that happens on earth. One of such principles is that of fatherhood. Anyone who is a father or desires to become a father must learn these principles, if he desires to be a better father. So what are these principles of fatherhood and what do they accomplish in the lives of others, especially the children they father? To begin with, according to Dr. Myles Munroe;

"Purpose is inherent in everything that has been created."

He goes on to expatiate the difference between the physical, mental, psychological and dispositional nature of the male and female is providential, essential, valuable and necessary for the fulfilment of their particular purpose in life. Most importantly, **God intended men to be fathers**. That was the primary reason God created men, and He designed men to eventually be fathers. Fatherhood is therefore the ultimate purpose of any good father.

In his book, *The Principle of Fatherhood,* Dr. Myles Munroe spells out the functions of fathers. He gives functional synonyms of the title father, thus: **Source, Nourisher, Sustainer, Supporter, Founder and Protector, Progenitor, Ancestor, Founder, Author, Teacher** and **Creator.** From the above functional titles, the word *father* is not so much a name but a title resulting from a function.

WHAT ARE FATHERS FOR?

GOD IS THE SOURCE OF ALL CREATION and He is our Father through our creation as well as our redemption in Jesus the Christ. Indeed, we are restored to Him as Father through the sacrifice of His Son, Jesus Christ, the "Everlasting Father" who produced a new generation of human beings.

According to Dr. Myles Munroe, "*Jesus Christ, God the Son, is the Essence, the very Being of the Father. Just as God is the Father of all living things, He made Adam to be the father of the human family.*" Indeed, men are distinguished in their role of father in many ways especially in the following:

a) The male is the source of seed;

b) The male is the nourisher of fruit;

c) The male is the source of the female;

d) The male is designed to protect his fruit;

e) The male determines the type of the offspring and influences its quality;

f) The male maintains his offspring;

g) The male teaches his seed.[3]

Now, back to the question: **what are fathers for?** In almost half many households with children, mothers are the sole or primary breadwinners. This victory for working women shows evolving family economics — or maybe, two very different types of families. So what is the purpose of men in modern families? Do fathers bring anything unique to the table?

"CHILDREN ARE BETTER OFF WITH A FATHER THAN WITHOUT ONE"

This was a title of an article written by W. Bradford Wilcox, the director of the National Marriage Project at the University of Virginia. He is the author of *"Gender and Parenthood: Biological and Social Scientific Perspectives."* It was published online and updated on December 16, 2013, 4:30 PM. I quote him verbatim here:

"It can be tempting - in a world where women are increasingly likely to be single mothers, "breadwinner moms" or supermoms seemingly able to do it all - to think of men as superfluous to the family. From Hollywood to academia, this view has tremendous currency. In "Raising Boys Without Men," for instance, the Cornell psychologist Peggy Drexler put it this way: "women possess the innate mompower that in itself is more than sufficient to raise fine sons."

---

[3]Source: *The Fatherhood Principle,* Dr. Myles Munroe. Chapter 1

But the view that men are superfluous in today's families is dead wrong. While it is certainly true that some children raised without fathers turn out just fine, on average, girls and boys are much more likely to thrive when they have the benefit of a father's time, attention, discipline and especially affection.

Boys are more likely to steer clear of trouble with the law when they grow up with their father in the home. One Princeton study found that boys raised apart from their fathers were two to three times more likely to end up in jail before they turned 30.

Dads matter for daughters as well. Another study found that girls whose fathers disappeared before the girls turned 6 were about five times more likely to end up pregnant as teenagers than peers raised with their fathers in the home.

And we know that kids — especially boys — are more likely to excel in school, and to steer clear of the principal's office, when they are raised in a home with a father who takes their homework and school conduct seriously. So, even though many men cannot or need not serve as the primary breadwinners in their families, modern couples need to recognize that fathers' contributions to their children's welfare extend well beyond money.

President Obama it well: "Of all the rocks upon which we build our lives, we are reminded … that family is the most important. And we are called to recognize and honor how critical every father is to that foundation. They are teachers and coaches.

They are mentors and role models. They are examples of success and the men who constantly push us toward it."[4]

---

[4]© 2015 The New York Times Company

REFLECTIONS

- What are the principles of fatherhood?
- Do dads matter in the life of their daughters?
- Are there any benefits for daughters when their fathers dote on them?
- How do fathers instil confidence in their daughters particularly?

CHAPTER 6

THE PROCESS OF UNMASKING THE MASCULINE CODE

"We need the iron qualities that go with true manhood. We need the positive virtues or resolution, of courage, of indomitable will, of power to do without shirking the rough work that must always be done."

- **THEODORE ROOSEVELT**

I BELIEVE THAT THERE IS A ROADMAP to manhood and onto fatherhood. The 21st Century Man must know more about himself and understand himself before he could embrace responsibility and be a good father and a mentor. That roadmap is what I want us explore in this important chapter. Permit me to begin by stating categorically that, as a man, you had no control over being born *male*. But becoming a *man* – by living the ageless code of manhood – is a choice. It has always been so. As long as you have been born male, it is your choice to learn how to live as a man and be the male the Creator designed you by nature to be.

In ancient times, the decision to follow *the way of men* was essentially made for you by the leaders of the communities. The survival of tribes and clans depended wholly upon *all* men striving to become a *"real man"* by fulfilling some basic, uncompromised essentials such as: *protecting, procreating,* and *providing.* These three virtues were among the most basic functions of every man. This was not duties a young man was deemed qualified enough to execute. You needed to have gone through the process of responsibility in order the qualify to be a protector, a husband, a father, a mentor and a provider.

All who were called men in those days, were expected to *hunt* and to *fight* to *defend* the community. In a harsh environment, a man could not survive alone, and so could not afford to become an outcast. A man therefore had to learn to bond with fellow men in the community. A man had to belong to the army or a group of men to be able to boldly carry out his duty as a man and a father. This valuable asset to a community, we lack it big time in today's urban and suburban communities of cities and metropolis.

In the ancient time – and even in certain tribal communities existing today - beyond a concern for physical safety, a man's identity was so tied up with his tribe that to lose his status was emotionally crippling, and a big blow to his pride. Therefore, men in tribal communities would do anything to avoid this social isolation at all costs. Thus our primitive ancestors were highly motivated to try to pull their own weight and meet their community's standards of honour. How do we contrast this in our 21st Century world? Think about this.

Truth is, the decision of whether or not to strive for the traditional standards of manhood is not of recent origin. It is something men have grappled with ever since the first rays of civilization began to dawn. It began way back in the days of Adam, when he had to raise his many sons. This had run through the centuries and generations. As life became more comfortable, men were faced with the question of how much of the old, primitive ways to hold onto, and how much to surrender to the emerging comforts and luxuries of settled society.

Historically, some of the first people to wrestle with how to live as men in a more domesticated landscape were the ancient Greek and Roman philosophers. They pondered and debated what constituted the good life for a man. The Stoics for example, argued that it could be found in fighting their society's emerging trend towards softness and decadence and deliberately cultivating one's ruggedness and virtue.

Many of the great Stoic philosophers happened to be extremely rich and powerful men - Seneca was the tutor and advisor to the emperor Nero, and Marcus Aurelius was emperor himself. They could have helped themselves to all the indulgences their culture had to offer. Yet despite the temptation of being surrounded by wealth and luxury, these men *purposely* chose to take a different path from their peers. They chose *the hard way* of mental and physical toughness.

WHAT IS STOICISM?

Let me divert a bit to explain who a stoic is. A stoic is a person who practices stoicism and stoicism is an ancient branch of philosophy. Stoicism was one of the four principal schools of philosophy in ancient Athens - alongside Plato's Academy, Aristotle's Lyceum, and Epicurus' Garden, where it flourished for some 250 years. Stoicism was practiced mostly by men.

Stoicism proved especially popular among the Romans and attracted admirers of varied backgrounds. The statesman Seneca, the ex-slave Epictetus, and the Emperor Marcus Aurelius are examples. The works of these three authors have come down to us and have won admirers from the Renaissance through to the present day.

Although the philosophy of Stoicism as a whole is complex, embracing everything from metaphysics to astronomy to grammar, the works of the three great Roman Stoics focus on practical advice and guidance for those trying to achieve well-being or happiness. Here are four central ideas:

- **VALUE:**

According to stoics, the only thing that is truly good is an excellent mental state, identified with virtue and reason. This is the only thing that can guarantee our happiness. External things such as money, success, fame and the like can hardly bring us happiness.

Although there is nothing wrong with pursuing money, pleasure and happiness, and they do hold value and may well form part of a good life, often the pursuit of these things actually damages the only thing that can bring us happiness: an excellent, rational mental state. This is a mindset of many men, even today.

- **EMOTIONS**:

According to stoics, our emotions are the project of our judgements. Our emotions are influenced by our thinking, and indicates to us if something good or bad is happening or is about to happen. Many of our negative emotions are based on mistaken judgements, but because they are due to our judgements it means they are within our control. Change the judgements and you change the emotions.

Despite the popular image, the stoic does not repress or deny his emotions; instead he simply does not have them in the first place. That means, he has gone through a process to suppress his emotions systemically for a long time that it seems he has no emotions at all. This is not as cold as it might at first sound. What it means is, we ought to overcome harmful, negative emotions that are based on mistaken judgments, while embracing correct positive emotions, replacing anger with joy, sadness with satisfaction, hopelessness with positive mental attitude and believing in future prospects.

- **NATURE**:

Stoics suggest we ought to live in harmony with nature. Part of what they mean by this is that we ought to acknowledge that we but small parts of a larger, organic whole, shaped by larger processes that are ultimately out of our control.

Thus, there is nothing to be gained from trying to resist these larger processes except anger, frustration, and disappointment. While there are many things in the world that we can change, there are many others we cannot and we need to understand them or accept it.

- **CONTROL**:

In the light of what we have seen, there are some things we have control over – including our judgements, and our own mental state - and some things that we do not have control over – such as external processes and objects. Much of our unhappiness is often caused by confusing these two categories: thinking we have control over something that ultimately we do not. Happily, the one thing we do have control over is the only thing that can guarantee a good, happy life.

AS MEN OF THE 21ST CENTURY, we can learn a lot of lessons from the ancient stoics. We need self-control, ability to delay gratification and the ability to possess self-satisfaction. When today's man learns to live like a stoic, he is able to control himself, live a life of discipline and focuses on the major things in life and not easily distracted by minor, unnecessary things.

The Stoics devoted much of their time and energy to developing the ability to remain calm and collected in the face of adversity, as well as cultivating an indifference to pain, fear, avarice, and social approval. They intentionally sought out the kind of challenges their peers avoided. Cold baths, strenuous exercise, wearing plain and sometimes rough clothing, eating simple, and even deliberately seeking out ridicule were all methods Stoic philosophers practiced and encouraged other men to adopt. They believed this was the most fulfilling way to live – the only way to grow and progress.

FAST FORWARD TO TODAY. The amount and availability of luxuries has increased several times over. But despite our entry into the 21st Century, the modern man is essentially faced with the very same decision as the ancient brethren: How much should you indulge in the ease and comfort around you, and how much should you keep yourself apart and maintain your independence, mental sharpness, and physical toughness? Should you take the path of least resistance, or the hard way?

There is hardly anything in our current civilization that will complement to live the ancient and universal code of manhood. If you wish to live the way of men, you will, just as the Stoics did, have to intentionally choose to buck the tide of our culture, exercise your agency, and decide to live it yourself.

Without some outside force coercing them to live the code, most modern men will follow the path of least resistance and not even try. Naturally, this has and continues to produce social problems in regards to men that governments and pundits wring their hands about.

Doing so in our comfortable and luxurious world requires self-will and inner-discipline. It will require you to be proactive. Instead of expending your energy to complaining about today's cultural attitude dismissing the value or discouraging manliness, you will need to channel it into swimming against the tide, building yourself into a Superman, creating a familial tribe, and surrounding yourself with fellow men of honour.

Though the task is not easy, because a man who lives the code now does so of his own freewill and accord, rather than because he is compelled by an outside force, this path has never been more satisfying and fulfilling.

How do we resolve the cultural discord we have when it comes to manhood? We do not really need all 21st Century men in our current safe and luxurious environment. But what happens when things get rough and manly men are once again needed? Will we have men who have what it takes to protect and do the hard and dirty work necessary to keep things going? Can living a code of manliness actually enhance our lives and provide a deeper sense of satisfaction and fulfilment than would otherwise be possible?

There is an unmistakable parallel that keeps popping in my head as to how to resolve and explain this conflict we have in modern society when it comes to manhood, and that is the military reserves. Many militaries around the world have a *reserve force*. It's an organization of military personnel who are not full-time soldiers, but have undergone basic training and make a commitment to developing and maintaining their military skills so that they are ready to deploy should their country need them.

My proposal to resolving to the conflict of modern manhood is something akin to this model of service. We'll call it the Manhood Reserve. While abiding by the traditional code of manhood isn't urgent in our current environment, someday it might be and we'll need men prepared for that moment. Even if our society is not hit with some kind of crisis or catastrophe, our training in the Manhood Reserve will still be worthwhile.

We will all encounter hard times in our own lives that require the fortitude and strength that living the traditional code of manhood develops. Living the code will allow men to both scratch the itch of their original masculinity and achieve what the Greeks called *eudemonia*. That is the ancient Greek ideal of a life of excellence and full flourishing.

What follows is a framework that lays out the broad principles and specific training course pursuant to an enlistment in the Manhood Reserve. It seeks to wed tradition to the realities of modernity in order to create a pathway that both reach back and move men forward. It is positive and proactive. Joining up is voluntary and can be done by any man, in any circumstance, in any time. It does not require the culture around you to change or women to change. It is only dependent on you and your desire to live a manly life – what in Latin is termed *semper virilis* (always manly).

A CLASSIC EXAMPLE: THEODORE ROOSEVELT

Theodore Roosevelt was born into a wealthy family in New York City, USA. The Roosevelts enjoyed comforts and conveniences in the 19th Century that most Americans would not see until several decades later. When the Civil War tore America apart, Theodore's father had more than enough money to pay for a substitute and thus avoid a draft into the Union Army.

Roosevelt could have easily settled into a life of cosmopolitan comfort. But, young Theodore Roosevelt chose a different path for himself. He chose the hard way. What he called *"the strenuous life"* In Theodore's time, diligence and *being a good man, was the expected code* and Roosevelt kept this code. But he did not want to just be a good man, he wanted to be good at being a man, too. It was a goal he actively pursued.

Theodore spent his adolescence exercising and building up his once frail body. He took up boxing in college and became a competitive fighter. During winter breaks in school, he would go up to Maine and hunt with the famous guide and timber-man by name Bill Sewell. Then a tragic event in his life occurred. He lost both his wife and mother to death on one night. An extraordinary tragedy, enough to *break* any man, but not Theodore. After a grieving period, instead of continuing to wallow and despair, Roosevelt headed out to the badlands of the Dakotas to take up cattle ranching.

Roosevelt quickly earned the respect of rough and hard cowboys by showing he could pull his own weight and was not afraid to jump into the fray. He cleared out stables himself without complaint. He captured a company of horse thieves after tailing them for three days in sub-zero weather. He knocked out a gun-wielding loudmouth with three dynamite punches. By striving to live the hard way in his younger years,

Roosevelt armed himself with the fire and fight he needed to succeed later in the political, social, and intellectual challenges of his later life.

Even as a middle-aged U.S. President, Roosevelt did not relent on his dedication to testing himself and living the arduous life. He took part in judo and boxing matches in the White House. He interspersed his schedule with hunting and brisk hikes. He stayed ever-ready for whatever adventures and exploits might await him. He was indeed a man of great exploits.

Roosevelt served as police commissioner, governor, assistant secretary of the navy, and ultimately, President – and the youngest ever to assume the office. When war broke out with Spain in Cuba, Roosevelt put together his own volunteer unit and led them in a charge. He was a devoted husband and father of six children. He read extensively and authored thirty-five books of his own! After his days as President were over, he set out on an expedition to explore an uncharted part of the Amazon River and nearly died in the process.

Throughout his life, Theodore Roosevelt had the choice to reject the masculine code, but he never did. He sought to ever challenge himself *"in the arena"* and to always *"carry his own pack."* – quoting his own words. Some historians comment on Roosevelt's obsession with the strenuous life to a symptom of the *"male anxiety"* that many 19th Century urban men faced in America. It was the age of machines and steam and a man's place in society was being questioned. Questions like "what was the use of masculine strength when new machines could do the work of twenty men?" and "with the frontier closed, what use was there for the old pioneer qualities of ruggedness and self-reliance?"

ANY LESSONS FOR TODAY'S MAN?

Roosevelt and other men of his time ignored the hand-wringing and deliberately chose to live by the code of men, even though it was not demanded of them. That is why I admire great men like Theodore Roosevelt. He showed us a good example. His life story teaches men of today that it is possible to live in our modern world of luxury and comfort, but not be softened by it. He showed us that you could proactively choose to be good at being a man even when your surroundings or culture aren't conducive to exercising your innate masculinity.

Theodore Roosevelt showed us that it is possible to live *in* civilization but not be *of* it. As you read now, my dear reader, probably you are asking *"why?"* you might be thinking, why do I have to bother guiding my life by an idea of manhood that was formed in another time in history and is no longer suited for our modern, hi-tech, internet driven, techno-industrial world? Why do I have to live like a man when I would not necessarily be honoured for it?

While living the code of man might primarily have been about what you got from others in return, today it is something you need only to do for yourself. If you are looking for pats on the back, turn back now! Be the man you were created to be. Set good examples for the younger generation to follow. Raise boys. Mentor boys and develop them into men of purpose.

LIVE THE MASCULINE CODE and it will enormously benefit your family, your community, and ultimately, your nation - even if you are not recognized or celebrated for the great roles you play in your own small way. Those you mentor well will appreciate you – even if not all of them, one out of ten will come back to say 'thank you' or go out there and live a great life, citing you as his mentor and inspirer of his success!

Your good example will lead to friendships with other great men, and assuredly make you more attractive to women and the society at large. It is also simply the best way to live your own life, regardless of whether or not anyone else notices or cares. You are a man. This is what you were made to do. Embrace it. Be ready always. Be a real man who is good at being a man. Today's world needs men who are shaped and moulded by the ancient ideal of manliness!

I do not know about you, but I want to be able to look my wife and kids in the eye and say with boldness: **"I'll love you, protect you, provide for you and take care of you"** and mean it! I would also want to surround myself with other good and responsible men, who are also good at being men and are brothers indeed, and put our shoulders together and carry the responsibility of being effective men, husbands and fathers to our children! We must be able to become the number one role models and mentors in the lives of our children.

WE MUST BE MEN OF CHARACTER, before we display ourselves as men of charisma! Together, we must put our hands on the wheel and raise godly children and re-build our world together! That is what I define as fulfilment: good men raising great men, who will carry the mantle of masculine responsibility and effective fatherhood to the next generation!

FIND A BALANCE AMONG THE THREE P'S

You remember the Three P's I introduced earlier in this chapter? Yes, a true man has many functions or duties to his generation, and the three key ones among them are: Protect, Procreate, and Provide. I term these, the Three P's of True Manhood. Are you are man thinking about crafting your own roadmap to manhood in this 21st Century? Then keep in mind these Three P's of Manhood: Protect, Procreate, and Provide. Remember that each of them is a pillar that holds the home, the family, the community and the society at large. When the home crumbles, the whole society crumbles as well. When men as fathers take good care of their homes and mentor their children well, society benefits greatly.

It may be tempting to focus on the pillar of manhood that appeals to you the most, but you do so at your own peril. As we have noted throughout the chapter, when one or two of the P's of Manhood are weakened or non-existent, greater stress is placed on the remaining pillars, causing them to twist and get warped. Like the leaning tower of Pisa, society would lean as if about to fall, when all the three are not working together, interacting with each other dynamically.

We must become what the men of the ancient times called a *"Complete Man."* That requires developing each pillar of the 3P's to your fullest capacity in order to ensure that there is a good balance with one another. Building all three pillars of your manhood awakens all the dimensions of your original masculinity, and ensures that all of your human potentials are harnessed, deployed and maximized. This leads to a fulfilling life of a true man.

REFLECTIONS

- What are the benefits of men learning to bond with fellow men in the community?
- It is important for a man to belong to a group of men to be able to boldly carry out his duty as a man and a father. Why?
- List the qualities that makes a man a *Complete Man*

CHAPTER 7

BAR MITZVAH: TRANSISTION FROM BOY TO MAN

"Sometimes the poorest man leaves his children the richest inheritance."

- **RUTH E. RENKEL**

MANHOOD IS MORE THAN just physical size and maturity. Therefore, transitioning from a boy to a man is not only a privilege but a great responsibility as well. Transitioning from a boy to a man is a process and not an event. The best gift a dad can ever give his teenage son is the roadmap to manhood, and that calls for a ceremony of a sort. Among the Jewish people, such a ceremony is called *Bar Mitzvah*.

The simple meaning of the word *mitzvah* actually is *command*. It appears in various forms with that meaning about 300 times in the first Five Books of the Bible. For example, the Talmud mentions that the Jewish People were given 613 *mitzvot* at Mount Sinai, and many more numerous codes. In common usage, a mitzvah often means *"a good deed."* The Jerusalem Talmud commonly refers to any charitable act as *"the mitzvah."*

Often the word *mitzvah* is related to the Aramaic word *tzavta*, meaning to *attach* or *join*. *Tzavta* can mean companionship or personal attachment. In this sense, a mitzvah bundles up the person who is commanded and the Commander, creating a relationship and essential bond. Although, the term *"mitzvah"* seems to apply only to those activities that Jewish people celebrate, the term is applied as well to seven rabbinical mitzvot, namely:

1. *Washing hands for bread.*
2. *Laws of Eruv.*
3. *Reciting a blessing before partaking of food or any other pleasure.*
4. *Lighting Shabbat candles.*
5. *Celebration of Purim.*
6. *Celebration of Chanukah.*
7. *Recitation of the prayer of praise called Hallel on certain occasions.*

For each of these, there are blessings which begins exactly the same as a blessing said over a Torah mitzvah: *"Blessed are You, Lord our God, King of the Universe, who has sanctified us with His commandments and commanded us...."* the Torah explicitly requires us to listen to the sages, but regard God's Word higher over their commands. The deepest expressions of the Divine Will are those acts which God expressly tell us to do in His Word. The Jewish communities derived their truths through studying and the celebration of The Torah. It is hard to keep up the performance of mitzvot without a renewable source of inspiration. Mitzvot is observed with joy and enthusiasm to lift a person a step above the world and have an enormously greater impact on the person's environment. Again, the key is study and communal participation.[5]

WHAT IS BAR MITZVAH?

The Hebrew word for bar*mi ṣwâ,* simply means *son* in the English language. *Barmiz·vah* (bär mĭts'və) in Judaism, considers a Jewish male of at least 13 years of age an adult and responsible for observing religious law. The ceremony is to recognize a boy as a bar mitzvah.[6]

Bar mitzvah is therefore a ceremony – akin to rite of passage, as similarly practiced in Ghana, the Dipo ceremony among the Krobos. Bar Mitzvah is undergone by a Jewish boy when he is 13 showing that he is now a full member of the Jewish community. The event is usually celebrated in a synagogue.

The most significant part of the ceremony is when the father blesses his child, connecting him to the covenant blessings of Abraham, and releasing him unto a life of responsibility. Indeed, the *bar mitzvah* is a major event in the life of a Jewish family. The young person works for years to prepare for it, and the family saves and plans for just as long.

---

[5] Reference: Rabbi Tzvi Freeman, a senior editor at Chabad.org, head of Ask The Rabbi team.

[6] Reference: American Heritage Dictionary of the English Language, Fifth Edition. Published by Houghton Mifflin Harcourt Publishing Company.

A *bar mitzvah* (for a boy) or *bat mitzvah* (for a girl) falls sometime around the 13th birthday, and it marks the beginning of ritual adulthood. That is, once a Jew has reached that age, they are responsible for themselves in keeping the commandments and participating in Jewish life.

FACTS ABOUT BAR/BAT MITZVAH[7]

- A Jewish man is *bar mitzvah* when he passes his 13th birthday, whether he has a ceremony or not.
- A Jewish woman is *bat mitzvah* at 12 years, 6 months, or at 13, depending on the custom of her community.
- The plural of bar mitzvah is *bnei mitzvah*.
- Jews of this age are responsible to know right from wrong, and to be responsible for their duties as a Jew.
- The customs surrounding *bnei mitzvah* celebrations differ from community to community.
- Preparation and study for a *bar mitzvah* begin years ahead of the actual date.
- Some adults who did not have the opportunity to celebrate their *bnei mitzvah* as 13-year-olds study for a similar celebration later: these are commonly called adult *bnei mitzvah*.

---

[7] Reference: Rabbi Ruth Adar, a teaching rabbi based in San Leandro, California, USA. Taken from Rabbi Ruth Adar's blog Coffee Shop Rabbi (https://coffeeshoprabbi.com/).

BAR MITZVAH, KNIGHTHOOD AND BIBLICAL MANHOOD

For an effective vision for manhood, a boy maturing into manhood must go through a process and that process requires some basic insights. As part of the process, we need to motivate and inspire our sons to live lives of honour and dignity. A lot of fathers struggle a lot in leading their sons into balanced, biblical masculinity.

C. S. Lewis wrote that there is a different strand of manhood. Made of a battle between fierceness and gentleness. He advises that we need "to find healthy synthesis in the person of the knight and in the code of chivalry. Here these competing impulses - normally found in different individuals - find their union."

According to Lewis, strength and power, without tenderness, for example, give us the brute. Tenderness and compassion without masculine firmness and aggressiveness produce a male without the fire to lead or inspire others. Biblical examples of these two elements resident in one man are many. For example, Jesus Christ, our Lord, revealed both tough and tender aspects in His humanity. He was a Lamb and a Lion. At one time, the Lord Jesus expressed a desire to gather the citizens of Jerusalem together as a hen gathers her young under her wings (Matthew 23:37).

JESUS CHRIST WEPT AT LEAST TWICE. Once at the tomb of Lazarus (John 11) and again as He looked out over the city of Jerusalem and reflected on the fate of those who rejected His witness (Luke 19:41-44). However, Jesus could also be very strict. Once He made a whip, ran off the money changers in the temple area, and turned over their tables (John 2:13-16). And, in the Garden of Gethsemane, His mere glance knocked grown men to the ground (John 18:6).

We also see in Apostle Paul, the same blend of firmness and gentleness. For example, he poured himself out tenderly nurturing his spiritual children (I Thessalonians 2: 5-9), but he endured more hardship than most soldiers (I Corinthians 11:23-27) and he did not hesitate to castigate false teachers (Galatians 5:12).

In the Old Testament, we see David, who was a poet and psalmist. He was also a warrior and a king of Israel. He had the fierceness to kill Goliath, the giant, and the tenderness to provide for the needs of Jonathan's descendants after Jonathan was killed – notable among them, Mephibosheth.

Keeping the right balance between our innate impulses toward power and aggression and the need to be gentle and tender is a challenge most men face. So at Bar Mitzvah, this must be borne on mind. In his book, *raising a Modern-Day Knight,* author Robert Lewis made it clear that Christian fathers can use *knighthood* as a symbol, or an ideal, and a metaphor for guiding their sons into authentic manhood. In this way opposing drives can be harnessed and balanced.

Of course, everyone experiences difficulty balancing competing impulses, but it is specifically the violence by young males that is bringing our society to the verge of breakdown. Our young men need a vision for masculinity that challenges and inspires them. For our society to be stable and healthy, we need men who have developed both their tender side as well as the fierce side and can balance the two. In an age of great social, spiritual, and gender confusion, such as ours, there is a desperate need for clear guidelines and models that can inspire young men and harness their aggression for constructive ends. This is where the image of *the knight* comes into the picture.

Since the Middle Ages knights in iron have fired the imaginations of young men. Knighthood is attractive because of its code and its call to courage and honour. Young men are intrigued by testing themselves against various standards, and the code is inspiring because of its rigour and strictness.

THERE IS A NEED FOR MODERN-DAY KNIGHTS

In his enthusiastic foreword to Robert Lewis's book, *Raising a Modern-Day Knight,* Stu Weber writes: "Our culture is in deep trouble, and at the heart of its trouble is its loss of a vision for manhood. If it's difficult for you and me as adult males to maintain our masculine balance in this gender-neutral culture, imagine what it must be like for our sons, who are growing up in an increasingly feminized world."[8]

We must supply our young men with healthy, noble visions of manhood, and the figure of the knight, in this regard, is without equal. In the knight we find a conception of manhood that can

---

[8] Stu Weber cited in Robert Lewis, *Raising A Modern-Day Knight: A Father's Role in Guiding His Son to authentic Manhood* (Colorado Springs, Colo.: Focus on the Family, 1997), vii.

lift, inspire, and challenge our young men to new heights of achievement and nobility. Matthew Bennett, in "The Knight Unmasked," *The Quarterly Journal of Military History*, Vol. 7, no. 4 (Summer 1995):10, cited in Robert Lewis, *Raising a Modern-Day Knight*, 18. He asserted that: "*Not all knights were great men, but all great men were knights.*" According to Will Durant, chivalry and knighthood gave to the world one of the "major achievements of the human spirit."

C. S. Lewis, in his essay, "The Necessity of Chivalry," agreed. He wrote that the genius of the medieval ideal of the chivalrous knight was that it was a paradox. That is, it brought together two things which have no natural tendency to gravitate towards one another. It brought them together for that very reason. It taught humility and forbearance to the great warrior because everyone knew by experience how much he usually needed that lesson. It demanded valour of the urbane and modest man because everyone knew that he was likely as not to be a milksop."[9]

Someone once said history teaches us that, *"When most men are soft, a few hard men will rule."* For this reason, we must do everything we can to build into our boys the virtues of strength and tenderness so they can be strong, solid family men and so society will be stable! The lack of connection between fathers and sons in most cultures of today, made worse by broken homes and the busyness of our lives, has left many young men with a *masculine identity crisis*. **Our sons are looking to their**

---

[9] C. S. Lewis, "*The Necessity of Chivalry*," 13-26.

fathers for direction. Fathers are searching for real answers in their attempts to guide their sons into godly manhood. I seek to provide answers and guidelines in this book.

As fathers, we have a way to point sons to manhood with clear ideals: a vision for manhood, a code of conduct, and an inspirational cause to pursue. The pattern of advancement from *page* to *knight* provides fathers with a logical process for guiding our sons into manhood. There are numerous suggestions for ceremonies that seek to equip dads with a variety of means to celebrate and validate their sons' achievements. Bar Mitzvah is a typical example.

Now let us turn our attention to the knight and his ideals. In *Raising a Modern-Day Knight,* author Robert Lewis suggests three major ideals for modern-day knights: a vision for manhood, a code of conduct, and a transcendent cause.

A VISION FOR MANHOOD:

The author Robert Lewis states in his book, four manhood principles and they are: Real men (1) reject passivity, (2) accept responsibility, and (3) lead courageously, and (4) expect the greater reward. He suggests that though men have a natural inborn aggressiveness, they tend to become passive at home and avoid social responsibility. These principles, if followed, prevent passivity from becoming a significant problem.

A CODE OF CONDUCT:

The code for modern-day knights comes from the pages of the Holy Bible. Author Robert Lewis lists 10 ideal characteristics appropriate for modern-day knights taken from the Holy Scriptures and they are: loyalty, kindness, humility, purity, servant-leadership, honesty, self-discipline, excellence, integrity, and perseverance.

Modern-day knights must be trained in three important areas. Firstly, the modern-day knight needs to understand that there must be a will to obey the Will of God, if there is to be spiritual maturity. The young man must come to know that life is intrinsically moral and that there is a God who knows everything and who rewards good and punishes evil.

He must know that absolute moral values exist and that the commandments of God are liberating, not confining. Lewis states "True satisfaction in life is directly proportionate to one's obedience to God. In this context, moral boundaries take on a whole new perspective: they become benefits, not burdens."

Secondly, the modern-day knight needs to understand that he has a work to do that is in keeping with his inner design. This work is not just his profession or trade, but refers to work in his home, church, and community. Life is certainly more than a job, and your son should hear this from you lest he get the mistaken perception that manhood is just one duty and obligation after another.

A third realm of responsibility for the modern-day knight is a woman to love. The code of chivalry requires that all women be treated with respect and honour. Sons need to see and hear from their fathers the importance of caring for women in general and loving, leading, and honouring their wives in particular.

The knight in training should be taught the value of work, have summer jobs, do chores around the house, and study hard on his school work. The goal here is to establish patterns of industry and avoid sloth-like behaviour so that a solid work ethic is in place as he gets older.

A TRANSCENDENT CAUSE:

Life is ultimately unsettled if it is lived solely for self. Jesus Christ said if you give up your life you will find it, so if you live for a cause greater than yourself, you'll be happy and fulfilled. A *transcendent cause* is a cause that a person believes is truly heroic - a noble endeavour calling for bravery and sacrifice, timeless – or has significance beyond the moment, and is supremely meaningful, but not useless.

The only antidote to the futility of life is a transcendent cause and a vision for life that "integrates the end of life with the beginning," and connects time and eternity. Obviously becoming a Christian, developing a personal relationship with Christ, and living for Him are basic, irreplaceable elements for having a meaningful life.

A KNIGHT GOES THROUGH CEREMONIES

Like the knight, let us now turn our attention and focus on the importance of ceremonies in the life of a young man. It is said that a knight remembers the occasion of his *dubbing* (that is his instalment as a knight) as the finest day of his life. Such is the power of ceremony, it makes celebrated events unforgettable. Ceremonies are also invaluable markers that state emphatically: "Something important has happened here!"

Older men have instinctively seen the wisdom of providing for their son's markers of their journey to manhood. These markers have been in the form of periodic ceremonies or a significant, final ceremony. Following such events there is no doubt in the young man's mind that he has reached the stage in his development celebrated in the ceremony. Later he can always look back on the ceremony and remember what it meant.

After an elaborate physical, social, mental, and religious disciplines endured and passed in relation to his *dubbing ceremony,* no medieval knight ever wondered, "Am I a knight?". Such matters had been settled forever by the power of ceremony in the presence of other men. This is what our sons need. Our sons do not normally have such experiences. As Lewis writes, "One of the great tragedies of Western culture today is the absence of this type of ceremony...I cannot even begin to describe the impact on a son's soul when a key manhood moment in his life is forever enshrined and memorialized by a ceremony with other men."[10]

Now, there are natural stages in a young man's life that lend themselves to celebration. Each stage has a parallel in the orderly steps toward knighthood. Let us find out how.

PUBERTY: THE PAGE CEREMONY:

The first step for a young boy on the path to knighthood was to become a page. He was like an apprentice, and he learned about horses, weapons, and falconry and performed menial tasks for his guardians. Since puberty occurs in a young boy's life around thirteen years and is an important point in a young man's journey toward adulthood, it is an excellent time for a simple ceremony involving the boy and his father celebrating this stage of the young man's life.

HIGH SCHOOL GRADUATION: THE SQUIRE CEREMONY:

The next stage on the path to knighthood was the squire; he was attached to a knight, served him in many ways, and continued to perfect his fighting skills. This stage is roughly parallel to the time of high school graduation. It should be marked by a more involved ceremony led by the boy's father but involving other men.

---

[10] Robert Lewis, *Raising a Modern-Day Knight*, 99.

ADULTHOOD: THE KNIGHT CEREMONY:

This is the stage in which *the squire*, after a period of testing and preparation, is dubbed a knight in an elaborate ceremony. This marks the end of youth and the arrival of adulthood for the knight. For the modern-day knight this stage of life is characterized by the completion of college or entering the world of work or military service.

The author suggests this stage as a perfect time to have a celebration marking a son's arrival at manhood and full adulthood. This ceremony should be very special; it should involve the young man, his father, his family, and other men.

In summary, we have been looking at Robert Lewis's book, *Raising a Modern-Day Knight*, and discussing knights and chivalry in an attempt to promote the knight as a worthy ideal, symbol, and metaphor for young men to emulate. A question left yet to be asked is why young men might need a stirring, vivid image or concept like the knight as a model. After a lifetime of studying cultures and civilizations, both ancient and modern, the eminent anthropologist Margaret Mead made the following observation:

> *"The central problem of every society is to define appropriate roles for the men."*

Margaret Mead is right! Author George Gilder adds a similar insight when he states: *"Wise societies provide ample means for young men to affirm themselves without afflicting others."* Yes, men need appropriate roles, and they need the desire to live and perform those roles. Men need to be inspired to do so. Men need roles that are considered valuable and held to be worthwhile.

This is true because men are psychologically more fragile than women and suffer with their identity more than women do, though some feminists would have us think otherwise. Why is this so? It is true because as one author puts it rightly "Men, more than women, are culture-made." This is why it is so important to have a culture-wide vision of manhood.

In modern Western society boys make the journey to manhood without a clear vision for what healthy manhood is. If they get out of control, the whole society suffers. Proverbs 29:18 states clearly: *"Where there is no vision, the people perish"*. Meaning, without vision, people are unrestrained. Knights and chivalry can supply a stirring vision of manhood that has been lacking. Yet some may think that the figure of the knight is an inappropriate image to use to inspire Christian young men. Such people need to take a close look at the Bible.

The teachings of Jesus Christ and the letters of Paul use the image of the hard working farmer, the athlete, and the soldier to illustrate the points they are trying to make. Additionally, there are numerous biblical passages that picture knight-like images, some of whom are angelic beings and others are Christ Himself. Specifically, the Book of Revelation is stuffed with images of courtly life familiar to medieval knights: kings, thrones, crowns, swords, censers, bows, armies, eagles, dragons, chariots, precious stones, incense, and what have you.

We are more indebted to the knightly virtue of chivalry than we realize. Many of the concepts and words have become part of our familiar vocabulary. It is from *chivalry*, for example, that we acquired the concept of the *gentleman* and our concepts of sportsmanship and fair play. It is no accident therefore that the decline in chivalry parallels the rise of taunting and the "win at any price" attitude among our sports figures.

If we are successful in inspiring our young men to seek to become modern-day knights, we need to remind them and ourselves that one cannot become a knight on his own. Our young knights need the company of godly men to be all that they can be. They need the tutorials. They need mentoring. They need role models. As Robert Lewis states it so well in his book:

> *"Boys become men in the community of men. There is no substitute for this vital component... if your boy is to become a man, you must enlist the community."*

Thus, if a father's presence is weighty, the presence of other men is weightier still, then enlisting the community of men will result in a depth of friendship that the lonely never experienced and the community of men keep expanding a son's spiritual and moral resources. This is what we need. This is the crusade I seek to launch in this book: that godly fathers should team up and together, we raise godly sons and daughters as our brand of 21st Century knighthood! Yes, we can and we must![11]

---

[11]NOTE: Most thoughts in this chapter reflect largely insights of Robert Lewis from his book, *Raising a Modern-Day Knight: A Father's Role in Guiding His Son to Authentic Manhood* (Colorado Springs, Colo.: Focus on the Family, 1997).

REFLECTIONS

- Is a *crying man:* a sign of weakness or strength?

- What is the best training ground for raising boys?

- Is it good to encourage boys to express their emotions?

CHAPTER 8

A CHRISTIAN MODEL OF MANHOOD

"It is easier to build strong children than to repair broken men."

- FREDERICK DOUGLAS

EVERY TEACHING ON MANHOOD must be based on the two most significant men in history: **Adam** and **Jesus Christ**. We all know what Adam did - or more precisely, what he did not do. When everything was on the line, he didn't take responsibility. He ducked behind Eve. Adam's failure was not just a moral failure; it was a failure of manhood.

Jesus Christ serves as the polar opposite to Adam. He faced challenges far greater than Adam, yet He held firm. His was a vision of faithfulness and nobility at all costs. Bringing together Adam and Jesus, we see that a good vision for manhood includes rejecting passivity, accepting responsibility, leading courageously, and expecting God's greater reward.

Sons need to hear this message from their fathers. Sons need words of encouragement, a focus on strengths instead of weaknesses. Sons need to hear how they can use their talents in positive, life-giving ways that match God's vision for manhood.

FORMING MANHOOD MODEL GROUPS

SONS NEED TO SEE FATHERS modelling manhood at home, especially with the son's mother. How a man interacts with his wife teaches the son how to act at home. The son will copy his father from the earliest years. The son is like a blank template, waiting to be pressed in the proper shape.

If you have a son and he is already in his teen years, or the relationship has been difficult, it's never too late for a fresh start. Sons want to connect to their fathers, no matter how old they are and no matter how badly you may have messed things up. If you have missed the mark with your son, now is the time to start anew. Go to a few Christian men for counsel. When the time is right, go to your son and apologize for letting your interests distract you from the relationship he needs with you.

Fathers, it is up to us to share the power of a Christian vision for manhood with our sons. Nature would not do it for you. Our culture will only deposit a false vision that leads to regret. Take responsibility for raising your son. If you do, you will someday know the satisfaction of watching your son drive off to college prepared - not just to take his classes seriously, but also to take the call to authentic manhood seriously.

We need to set up manhood-related small group programmes, where fathers and their sons meet. It should be non-denominational, Bible-based approach of building young men through the discipleship and mentorship of fathers. It should feature guided Biblical discussion with hands-on, interactive activities. Men can include other young men in their lives, such as nephews, neighbours or friends. Why do we need this?

My answer is simple: we live in a generation of *absentee fathers* and *non-involving fathers*. Many Dads have abandoned their son-shaping responsibility – physically, spiritually or relationally. This is taking a major toll on society: from stressed-out moms making up the difference to young men living confused and directionless lives. Manhood gatherings can help fathers be intentional and engaged.

A typical example of such a group usually consists of these: father-mentoring groups consist of 6 to 8 dads, who each bring their son(s). Young men without an engaged dad can also be brought by a caring man who wants to pour into their life. Groups meet for example, in 6-week sprints at a church or someone's home. Discussions are guided by *modules* that cover various topics. The young men are normally between the ages of 8 and 17 years of age.[12]

LET THE YOUNGER MAN KNOW HE HAS WHAT IT TAKES

Our teenagers live in a mixed-up society that bombards them with non-stop messages that tend to skew their perspectives on life. The predominant message in our society is that real manhood is all about the accumulation of power, celebrity

---

[12] Reference: Robert Lewis, the Executive Director of *Global Reach* and founder of *Men's Fraternity*.

status, possessions and prestige. No wonder most teenage boys are feeling under-equipped and just plain confused!

Young man, do not believe this *'tough guy'* façade. Teenage boys are scared they do not measure up to our culture's definition of manhood. There are not many safe places out there for boys. Boys at this age are notoriously vicious about putting each other down and exploiting any weakness. They get this vicious because they rarely get loved and affirmed, and they have lost identity and do not know who they really are. That makes them susceptible to deceptions and to many negative and even evil influences from friends and from online sources.

It's so important during those teenage years that our young men hear words of affirmation. We must let them know the journey of guided sonship is worth travelling, and that they need helpers and guides, who are genuine fathers, father-figures, coaches, guardians, role-models and mentors. They need words of affirmation and words of instruction. While they may be a very long way from manhood, hearing positive messages is crucial to any young man's development of self, and his maturation. Here are some examples of words of affirmations to use with your son:

"You're going to do great in this world because ..."

"You will make an awesome father someday because ..."

"You have amazing gifts to share with the world like ..."

"You're great, you are awesome, and you are incredible, because…"

It is easy to slip into negativity with your teenager because, quite frankly, teenage boys in particular can be frustrating and make you mad at times. But be patient and go the extra-mile to do your best to keep it positive! Invest yourself in them and tomorrow you will smile that you did!

MAKE SURE TO KEEP IT REAL

While teenage boys certainly need important affirmations from older men, be careful not to heap too much praise on him just to boost self-esteem. Teenage boys have big egos, yet they are very vulnerable and fearful within. They are no longer kids, but they are not yet adults too. So they find themselves pulled by both childhood tendencies and anticipated adult realities. Sometimes, a teenage boy suffers the pull of fearful fantasies and false flattery. That makes him confused. It is important therefore for dads to help them *"keep it real"* with their teenage sons. They need balance and being helped to be sober and to be moderate in the way they think.

During those teenage years, somebody needs to challenge the young men, and call them out to order. They need mature hands to guide them and help them make sense of things. They are prone to take the easy path in life, so a father guiding him to make key decisions in life is extremely helpful. Remember that, more often than not, your teen son will not ask you for help, yet when you offer help, wrapped in affirmation, they will most likely follow and obey. Even if he does not follow your exact advice, he will value it and apply it in whichever way suits him best. Always keep this in mind as you mentor the youth: **men are not just born, they are made.**

One more thing about teenage boys: they hate being controlled, manipulated or bamboozled. Teenage boys do not respect anything they get for free! So put 'price tags' on things you offer. Let them work for what you give them. Yes, they are gifts, but wrap it as work for them and encouraging them to 'pay' for it by performing a task and be rewarded by you.

TAKE HIM ON ADVENTURES

Note that, teenage boys yearn to be tested and pushed beyond the edge of their limits. Yes, young men enjoy a false sense of control, because most of the life they have grown up to experience can be accessed by the touch of a cell phone, or keystroke of a computer! Create activities that take the young man out of his comfort zones and into the world of the wild. These include extracurricular activities such as: cadet group work, boys' scouts, sports, robotics, music band, kid-teen's mentoring programmes, and youth camp or groups activities. These environments can teach valuable life lessons.

These are structured activities and handled by other men. To balance it, once in a while too, take them to men's group entertainment programmes, amusement parks, shopping malls, sports games, musical concerts, video games, etc. at all cost, ensure you take them to father-son activities, and at the end of the day, they would have good memories of their achievement. **Today's teenage boys need to encounter the wild, where life is unpredictable and anything can happen. Too many of today's fathers are so wrapped up in our kids' activities and enjoying our own personal comforts that we have forgotten to take our boys on adventures and teach them the lessons that only nature can teach. The opportunities to adventure are all around us: missions and evangelism trips, service projects, camping, fishing, surfing, hunting, hiking, marathon runs, etc. Seize those moments with your son! Just give your son the roadmap to manhood. Just be dad!**[13]

---

[13]Reference: Mike McCormick, author of *ManQuest: Leading Teenage Boys into Manhood,* a guidebook designed for fathers to have intentional conversations and engage in activities that help boys become men.

REFLECTIONS

- Make an *Action List* of at least 5 lessons you can teach your boy.

- How do you deal with broken promises with your children?

CHAPTER 9

THE FATHER AS A MENTOR

"These commandments that I give you today are to be upon your hearts. Impress them on your children. Talk about them when you sit at home and when you walk along the road, when you lie down and when you get up."

- **DEUTERONOMY 6:6-7 NIV**

THE DICTIONARY DEFINES A MENTOR AS a trusted counsellor or guide. A mentor is an individual, usually older, always more experienced, who helps and guides another individual's development. This guidance is done without thought of personal gain. Sam Mehaffie, in his book *Every Man's a Mentor*, defines a mentor as "a man willing to serve; to share his life with a boy; to be a role model, an encourager, a listener.

Mentoring helps to develop good character traits in a boy: fairness, decency, self-sacrifice, respect, loyalty, service, responsibility, integrity, unselfishness, honour, and self-esteem. And, when a godly man mentors a boy, he is helping to build Christian character into that boy, and hopefully will introduce him to Christ. A Christian mentor is a man reaching out to a boy to help him reach his God-given potential."

Can you name a person who had a positive and enduring impact on your personal or professional life, someone whom you would like to imitate? If so, then you already know what a mentor looks and feels like. As a Mentor Father to an abandoned boy, you have entered upon "holy ground" where God, your Heavenly Father, promises to be your Guide and Counsellor. He will give you wisdom and understanding to impart to this young boy godly wisdom and life-changing strategies to overcome his difficult family situation.

BECOMING A MENTOR

Today, the absence of fathers at home is among the number one social problems enveloping our homes and is challenging in many families across the world. Many sons are being raised from boys to men without the positive influence and impact of their fathers. So sad, right? That is why we need to unmask manhood and encourage the raising of many responsible fathers in the land!

The presence of a responsible father improves a variety of outcomes for children and serves as a protective factor against problem behaviours including teenage drug abuse, juvenile delinquency, teen pregnancy, truancy, and criminal activity. Supporting and encouraging fathers to become more present and actively involved in their child's life therefore offers significant potential to empower individual lives, and bless many foster families, and contribute to the overall well-being of the community and the nation at large.

Mentoring or having the presence of a positive father figure in the absence of a positively involved father has proven to be a powerful tool for helping many youths reach their full potential. In the Western world, there are well-established programmes and organizations that specifically address the need for more father-mentors. I believe we who live in Ghana and Africa can also do same and even do better. Yes, we can! We need more mentors and positive father-figures to provide more support, advice, counselling, friendship, reinforcement and constructive examples to what parents are already struggling to achieve.

WE NEED QUALITY MENTORING RELATIONSHIPS

Quality mentoring relationships offer significant potential to reduce the adverse effects of father absence by improving young people's attitudes toward parents, encouraging students to focus on their education, and helping children face daily challenges. Also, mentoring serves as an important means to promote responsible fatherhood via supporting and encouraging caring adults to become actively involved in the lives of children and youth.

Together, responsible fatherhood and quality mentoring offer hope to young lives through the power of presence. Whether you're interested in becoming a mentor, or connecting your child to mentoring programmes, learning more about what it means and ways to connect to a trustworthy programme are important first steps.

Let me end this chapter with an interesting story I read online, written by Mark Fields, who is the CEO at Ford Motor Company, in the USA. The article is titled: Lessons from My Greatest Mentor – My Dad, published on September 9, 2015 and I have produced it verbatim – with a little editing – below. Read it with keen mind and learn a few lessons in addition to what I have shared with you so far. It will enhance your knowledge about fathers as mentors to their sons.

LESSONS FROM MY GREATEST MENTOR – MY DAD

"If there's one trait I've practiced throughout my career, it's to never stop learning. Being a lifelong learner is part of developing yourself personally and professionally. In business - and in life - the most effective leaders take time to self-reflect and seek feedback. Having and being a mentor are great ways to gain a real-life education, and they can have a significant impact on your personal growth."

"Throughout my life, I've had several mentors who have helped shape me into the person I am today. Without question, my greatest and most influential mentor was my dad. My dad was my hero. He was a purchasing manager in a sprinkler company for most of his career and eventually went on to lead two companies in the conglomerate he worked for. From a very early age, he taught me the importance of setting high goals and working hard to achieve them. He always was giving advice - life advice and career advice."

"When I came into my first general manager position at Ford, he wrote me a handwritten letter. In the letter, he told me he was proud of my family and of the fact that I made something of myself. Yet what stands out most is the advice he gave me about being humble. He said:

"Just a word of caution to you, son. Today's success can turn rapidly to something different and not so nice – even though you are doing everything right. Keep your feet firmly planted on the ground and don't get carried away by your title or what's happening. And, if you do that, you will always be fine as a human being."

"TO THIS DAY, I carry his words with me - literally. I have four phrases on the back of my employee badge that reminds me of my dad's letter, his advice and the legacy he left. They are:

- *Be humble*
- *Be grateful*
- *Be positive*
- *Many depend on you*

"These four phrases remind me of the lens through which I need to view every opportunity, every challenge and every success. No matter where you are in your career — or your journey in life - sometimes, the most powerful lessons can be found in the simplest truths. A great mentor can provide straightforward feedback and advice to help you shape not only your career, but also your life."[14]

---

[14] Source: *Lessons from My Greatest Mentor* – My Dad, Mark Fields.

REFLECTIONS

- Can fathers mentor their sons?

- As a father, will you allow another man to mentor your son?

- If yes, what will be your criterion in selecting such a mentor?

CHAPTER 10

SEASON OF LIVING AS AN UNMARRIED MAN

"I wish that all men were as I am. But each man has his own gift from God; one has this gift, another has that. Now to the unmarried and the widows I say: It is good for them to stay unmarried, as I am."

- I CORINTHIANS 7:7-8

EVEN AS MARRIAGE IS A CHOICE, singleness is also a choice. Long before any man marries, he lives a life of singleness. Therefore, singleness can be a means to an end: marriage. In like manner, to some people, singleness is a choice to live all their lives without the company of the opposite sex in an intimate, sexual relationship. We have the Roman Catholic Church's priests and nuns as a major example. For the sake of their holy calling, priests and nuns choose to sign to a vow to live the rest of their lives as unmarried, unattached, and in single devotion to Christ and their holy calling. That is called the ministry of *celibacy*.

What does the Bible say about a Christian staying single? The question of a Christian staying single and what the Bible says about believers never marrying is often misunderstood. Paul tells us in I Corinthians 7:7-8: "I wish that all men were as I am. But each man has his own gift from God; one has this gift, another has that. Now to the unmarried and the widows I say: It is good for them to stay unmarried, as I am."

Notice that he says some have the gift of singleness and some the gift of marriage. Although it seems that nearly everyone marries, it is not necessarily God's will for everyone. Paul, for example, did not have to worry about the extra problems and stresses that come with marriage and/or family. He devoted his entire life to spreading the Word of God. He would not have been such a useful messenger if he had been married.

On the other hand, some people do better as a team, serving God as a couple and a family. Both kinds of people are equally important. It is not a sin to remain single, even for your entire life. The most important thing in life is not finding a mate and having children, but serving God. We should educate ourselves on the Word of God by reading our Bibles and praying. If we ask God to reveal Himself to us, He will respond (Matthew 7:7), and if we ask Him to use us to fulfil His good works, He will do that as well.

"Do not conform any longer to the pattern of this world, but be transformed by the renewing of your mind. Then you will be able to test and approve what God's will is - his good, pleasing and perfect will."

- **ROMANS 12:2**

Singleness should not be viewed as a curse or an indication that there is *"something wrong"* with the single man or woman.

Marriage is an institution and those who marry must first believe that marriage is for them, and have the desire and intention of entering into that institution. People marry for many legitimate reasons. In same manner, many choose a life of singleness for various legitimate reasons. As far as I am concerned, if one does not feel ready to marry, he must continue to enjoy singleness as best as he can.

While many people marry, and while the Bible seems to indicate that it is God's will for most people to marry, a single Christian is in no way a "second class" Christian. No! In I Corinthians 7, Apostle Paul addressed every sensitive issue on marital relationship, and singleness was one of them. The great apostle deemed singleness as *"a higher calling."* As with everything else in life, we should ask God for wisdom (James 1:5) concerning marriage. Following God's plan, whether that be marriage or singleness, will in the end, result in the productivity and joy that God desires for us.[15]

I believe that, marriage and the rearing of children are God's normal design and primary way for propagating the human race and transmitting spiritual and moral values from one generation to the next generation. Of course, I do also agree that, a great number of churches have elevated marriage and family so highly to the neglect of the special needs and challenges of those who choose singleness as their way of life.

---

[15]Recommended Resources: *Single Servings:* 90 Devotions to Feed Your Soul by Lee Warren & Logos Bible Software. www.gotquestions.org.

I respect persons who have taken a decision to dedicate their whole adult lives to be God's agent of help in other people's lives and therefore cannot marry and raise biological children. A classic example is Father Campbell of the Christ the King Church, Accra, Ghana. He has devoted over three decades of his life to ministering among persons living with leprosy, in addition to serving as priest in the church.

TYPES OF SINGLES

Today within our society singles exist for one of two reasons: by choice, or by circumstance. In either case the Bible's mandate is clear for all unmarried individuals: they are to *remain sexually pure* (I Corinthians 6:18-20). The church must come to the realization that, those who choose to live as singles are neither *"wrong"* or *"strange"* in doing so. In fact, there are many valid reasons for remaining single, and may include:

- *Lack of a qualified, compatible or suitable partner;*
- *An unwillingness to make necessary marital commitments;*
- *Commitment to a particular mission that consumes ones' maximum time;*
- *Physical and medical or hormonal problems etc.,*
- *Painful experience in the past, that has killed desire for sexual intimacy,*
- *Divorce and demise of partners;*
- *Having God's special calling of singleness on one's life.*

Apostle Paul discussed this last reason in his first letter to the Corinthians (I Corinthians 7:1-9). Paul had chosen to remain single, for the sake of the work of ministry God had called him into. He therefore viewed singleness as *a high calling* that freed him from divine obligations he would otherwise realize through marriage and parenting.

Paul himself therefore led a strictly celibate life all through his apostolic and missionary life. A celibate is someone who abstains from sexual intercourse and marriage. This obviously will be difficult for most of us, that is why one must have a calling into the life of celibacy and have the grace to live such a life, from God. For Paul, he saw singleness as a gift given by God to select people. He felt strongly that, as a single, he would have more time to devote to ministry – and he did achieve that admirably!

Nevertheless, Paul was fair in his teaching. He realized that majority of Christians were not called by God into such a ministry and suggested that they pursue marriage, in order to remain pure and not bring reproach on the Gospel. Admirably, but unfortunately, Paul's personal and unique gift of singleness has led some churches to require celibacy of its clergy. Roman Catholic Church in particular. However, on record, there is nowhere in the Bible that such a high standard is required of those who are called to serve as full-time ministers of God.

SINGLENESS IS A SPECIAL GIFT of the Holy Spirit to various individuals in the Body of Christ, and not necessarily to pastors or leaders. Many who choose celibacy, are not *single by choice* but rather through circumstances of life drive them to that choice. This group of people includes: the never married, the divorced, and those who are alone because of spousal death – such as widows and widowers.

Sadly, many in the church have not recognized the emotional and spiritual needs of singles. Neither have they realized the great ministry potential of being single. Although usually unintentional, this occurs for various reasons. For example, the most common reason is the predominance of married couples within the church, who inadvertently overlook singles and their needs.

Social events are planned with the assumption that men and women will come in pairs, either as married or dating couples. Therefore, singles, who need and desire fellowship, are often over-looked. In such cases singles feel left out and distance themselves from an occasion which should be edifying and supportive, and possibly, if this is their desire, could have opened a door for him or her to establish new friends which may well end in a marriage-bound relationship.

Now let us seek means to solve this issue, especially in our churches – considering that many Christians meet their partners in churches. Some churches have very effective and dynamic programmes that ensure singles are involved and not isolated. To provide the needs of singles a church can provide quality singles ministries, which offer emotional support and group fellowship. While such ministries are often effective in ministering to this vital segment of the church, they have simultaneously proven counter-productive in certain local settings.

For example, singles groups tend to focus primarily on one of four categories of people, namely: *never married youth, never married older adults, divorced spouses*, and *widowed adults*. Despite such groups of people, there is the presence of small children, teenagers, adult children and this makes the mix even more complex. It is further complicated by age and gender differences. This brings to question whether or not singles should be separated from the main body of believers. Many singles would say such separation only increases their isolation. What many singles want is acceptance and fellowship as adult equals in the Body of Christ.

Married persons often fail to realize that singles want to form friendships with married couples. Although married couples have common concerns that draw them together - cement marital relationships and rearing children in two-parent homes - they need to include singles, mutually sharing and receiving the love of Christ as appropriate to the age level and gender status.

Singles should be encouraged and helped to use their singleness for God. As Paul suggested, ministry can be more focused and intense when family obligations are not present. Singles who make this commitment and devote themselves to ministry should be respected by others in the church for their commitment to Christ. Though there may be situations in which a married couple can be more effective and less vulnerable to temptations, the church has the responsibility of providing singles the opportunity to bless, edify, and minister to others.

One category of Christians should never depreciate the gifting and role of other Christians. The rich should never despise the poor. The educated should never despise the uneducated. The less educated should never ignore those who have learned through diligent study. Singles should not depreciate those who are married, in like manner; the married should not ignore the singles.

Remember we are one in the Body of Christ (Galatians 3:26-28). We should be one in the bonds of Christian love and not look down on others or take advantage of each other. Single life can be beautiful and enjoyable. It is great to be a young, single man. If you are a single man, choose to live a pure life and at the same time enjoy the company of godly ladies or sisters in the church. Be honest with yourself and unto others.

If you are in the company of a lady or ladies that tempt you to compromise your virtues, change direction and leave that company wisely but hurriedly. Know that God will surely grant you a spouse that you will love and cherish. So enjoy life. Learn all you ought to learn about the opposite sex and about the art of marriage. Learn to know more about your body and its need. Learn self-control and delay gratification today.

Tomorrow when you are blessed with the wife you desire, you can then enjoy your union to the max, young man!

REFLECTIONS

- What are the two types of single men?

- How would you form a good relationship with a married couple?

- How would you form a good relationship with a single young man?

- Do you nominate a mentee or respond to a request from a mentee?

CHAPTER 11

BEING A MAN, A HUSBAND AND A FATHER

"Of all the rocks upon which we build our lives, we are reminded ... that family is the most important. And we are called to recognize and honour how critical every father is to that foundation. They are teachers and coaches. They are mentors and role models. They are examples of success and the men who constantly push us toward it."

- **PRESIDENT BARAK OBAMA**

MEN ARE NOTED FOR THEIR PLACE at the forefront, especially in management and leadership circles. We do excel as managers and leaders, especially in the corporate world. However, when it comes to the management and leadership of the home, most men as husbands and fathers are found wanting!

Let me state here before I go farther that, if as a man and a husband, you are into business, your mandate is not only to be a father to your own children; you are called and mandated by God to be a father in business as well. You have been placed strategically to raise godly leaders who exude integrity and diligence in their duties. You are called and positioned to be a Joseph and a Daniel at your workplace. Many have to look up

141

to you and not be disappointed as a manager, a leader or an ordinary worker.

As a Christian, you are called upon to be a salt wherever you work. As a believer working in a world that is ungodly, it is your duty to be the shining light that everyone looks up to. Unbelievers must look at your life and your integrity and desire to emulate you or at least your character attributes. Many are watching you daily and they are eager to see if your confessions are your real lifestyle. They want to know if your moral values are mere talk or real belief. Your character and lifestyle speaks louder than what you claim you believe!

SO THEN, THE QUESTION IS, what is the proper role of men in the family and society? History reveals extremes from the family dictator to the awkward passive dad. But what did God design? You know, society has many different ideas about what the role of men should be. But what does our loving Creator intend? What does the Good Book reveal on this matter?

To answer that question, we need to start in the beginning, at the creation of Adam and Eve. In Genesis 2 we see that Adam was created before Eve. Adam was given the task of naming all of the animals. It seems clear that at least part of the purpose for this was to help him realize that none of these creatures were "comparable to him." Every other creature had its mate; but Adam was at that point alone, the only one of his kind (Genesis 2:20).

After he naming all the animals, God then created a very special blessing for him: a woman fashioned from Adam's own rib. The connection between them was undeniable. Together they had oneness - they formed a family, a complete unit (Genesis 2:24).

In the New Testament, the Apostle Paul very specifically outlined the leadership roles God intended within the family in Ephesians 5:23. Here we see that the husband is to be the head of the wife *as* Christ is the head of the Church. That sets a very high standard for men to live up to! What specifically is this standard God expects men to live up to? Ephesians 5:25 makes two very important points. Firstly, Christ loved the Church, thus husbands are to love their wives unreservedly. Christ's love, in this context, represents an: "unselfish loyal and benevolent concern for the good of another" (Merriam-Webster's Collegiate Dictionary).

Secondly, **Christ gave Himself for the Church**. This is the demonstration of the authority or the head of the family to exercise a commitment to fulfil the needs of the family. Jesus Christ demonstrates this towards the Church. He shows real leadership and real love, and His kind of love is the unconditional, self-sacrificing one, that provides the felt needs of those He leads and loves. The husband here has an excellent Role Model to follow, when it comes to demonstrating unconditional love towards caring for the wife, children and the household.

The role of the husband is supposed to be one of *loving authority* and not a cruel *authoritarian* role. The husband as the head over the wife is called and empowered to exhibit a loving authority and not to be a dictator or master over his wife. The husband must always bear in mind that he is accountable to God for the welfare of his family. He is not called to only lead by meeting physical and financial needs. The God-kind of husband is mandated to as well provide leadership that is spiritual, moral, psychological and emotional.

Paul again reveals more of the husband's role as head of the household. We can find that in I Timothy 3. The general passage (reading from verses 1 to 13) is talking about the qualifications of *"bishops"* and *"deacons"* as leaders in the congregation of a local church. Ideally, these standards serve as benchmarks for most Christians to strive for. However, in this context, verses 4 and 5 state clearly that a leader should be one who "rules his own house well" and that his children must be in submission under his leadership. That is clearly a message for men and husbands who rule over their own households – before being chosen to serve as leaders in the house of God.

HUSBANDS ARE CALLED TO LIVE WITH WIVES IN UNDERSTANDING

THE APOSTLE PETER gives us further insight into the roles of godly husbands and fathers in I Peter 3:7. Here, husbands are instructed to "dwell with their wives with understanding, giving honour to the wife as to the weaker vessel, and as being heirs together of the grace of life." There are key points we can draw from this all-important verse. Let me begin by attempting to define the key words such as: *dwell, understanding, honour* and *weaker vessel.*

To begin with, the husband is instructed to "dwell with his wife with understanding." To dwell is to live, reside, settle, stay, inhabit, or to have or make a home. It takes the husband choosing consciously to live together with his wife, to turn a house into a home. So to dwell with your wife is a work and demands a sense of working together in harmony and in synergy. One spouse cannot make a home; it takes the husband and the wife to make a home, even before children are added by God's grace.

Understanding always walks together with knowledge and wisdom. There are many husbands who feel they can never "understand" their wives. Are you one of them? I agree in a way, because the make-up of a woman makes her more complex in being that the man. As Dr John Grey puts it in his book: *Men are from Mars, Women are from Venus.* God in His wisdom, created the woman to be a complement or completer of the man, thus, men and women do not have to be same to marry. They have to be different both in physical make-up as well as in the way they think and act. That is what gives us our unique masculinity and femininity.

However, as husbands, we have no excuse to keep saying our wives are complex so we cannot love them. It is our duty as men and as husbands to make sufficient and quality time to get to know our wives better and seek to "understand" them, first, as human beings, and as women, before we consider their roles in our lives as our wives.

Husbands, until you have made time to understand your wife as a human being and a unique woman, you can hardly appreciate her as your wife! One-on-one quality time together is indispensable, no matter how long you have to live together with your wife as a couple.

Adam in the Garden of Eden got so busy about his God-given business, leaving Eve alone most of the times. That gave room for the devil to use the serpent to engage her in constant conversations and the end result led to the fall of humankind. Women are primarily wired for companionship and conversation, so whoever grants them undivided attention, wins their hearts. Meditate on this!

Now, what of the phrase "weaker vessel" in the passage? Well, physically, women are generally smaller than men. Generally, a woman is not as physically strong as a man. Women are far more fragile than men, in their physique. So that was what God was directing husbands to consider carefully.

Apostle Peter by inspiration was advising husbands to take good care of their wives. Who are we to do that? We are mandated to look out for the best in our wives. We are to cherish them and to demonstrate tenderness toward them. We are instructed to be gentle on them and be patient with our women. Yes, we may never fully understand our women, but we can appreciate them and cherish them. Yes, we can!

You see, when God created the woman, He could have made her equal in strength and stature to the man, but He did not. Instead, He made them more fragile – as compared to how rugged and 'brute' we are designed as men. God has given us the responsibility as men, to protect, provide, preserve, cater for, care for, cherish and give honour to our wives.

Any man aspiring to be a godly and a good husband must make it a point to learn to hold his wife in high esteem. Even if you are unmarried, begin to learn how to use your masculinity to protect and cherish the women in your life – your mother, sisters, aunts, grannies, female friends and girlfriend, etc.

Finally, we are to take an important note of the truth that, as husbands, we are to cherish and honour our wives because we are "being heirs together of the grace of life." The Moffatt translation puts it this way: "**You must honour them as heirs equally with yourselves of the grace of life.**" This makes it clear that, we are both children of God in His Kingdom here on earth. As Christ, there is neither a man nor a woman. We are in same spiritual status before the heavenly Father: we are sons and co-heirs with Christ Jesus.

Of course, in His Church, God has established spiritual hierarchy or order of leadership, and both the man and the woman can be called to serve in key leadership roles - such as pastors, teachers, evangelists, prophets and apostles. So a husband could be called to serve in such a high capacity, while his wife is not. In same manner, a wife could be called, while the husband is not. But when it comes to the home, the leadership structure remains the same: the husband as head, the wife as the neck or supporter of his headship. Thus, a wife could be a bishop of a church, but at home, she remains a wife and nothing more or less!

Thus, the relationship between husband and wife should be harmonious and one of mutual love, mutual trust, mutual respect, and mutual understanding of each other's roles and functions in the union. We must know that both of us shall equally inherit eternal life and that we serve one Master: Jesus Christ. We must therefore submit to each other, love each other and serve each other with respect and in honour. By this, we shall create a godly and a happy home, that will be heaven on earth!

YOUR ROLE AS A FATHER TO BOTH YOUR WIFE AND CHILDREN

Do you know that a husband as a man is the father of the wife? Yes! In his position as a father, he is called by God to be a source and a covering unto his wife, even before they begin to make children. So a father operates a double-role, fathering his wife, first, then his children. Take good note of this truth.

Now, when a man marries and children start coming along, he enters a different phase of life. So it is important to ask: What is a man's responsibility toward his children? There is an old saying about fatherhood: **"The greatest gift a father can give to his children is to love their mother."** The family begins when a man and woman are joined as husband and wife.

The family grows from the two of them together, and the marriage relationship must remain the bedrock of the family. From infancy onward, children should be comforted by the close and loving relationship they see demonstrated between their mother and father. This gives stability to the family and credibility to the father as he goes on to properly teach and train his children.

YOUR RESPONSIBILITY AS A TEACHER

And teaching his children is a major responsibility of a father. Most important is to teach them the ways of God. In both Deuteronomy 6:7 and Deuteronomy 11:19 we find that parental instruction should be an ongoing process: "When you sit in your house, when you walk by the way, when you lie down, and when you rise up". While there should also be times of more formally teaching your children, the inference from these instructions is that teaching should be just a normal part of life. The father should live God's way of life and teach it to his children through everything he does and says all day long!

Abraham – as we shall consider in detail in the next chapter - was commended by God because of the example he set and the way he led his family. God knew Abraham would *"command his children and his household after him, that they keep the way of the LORD, to do righteousness and justice"* (Genesis 18:19). This responsibility applies to both parents and requires that they spend enough time with their children daily.

For a father, spending time teaching, guiding, playing with and working with his children has to be a priority. It is a God-given responsibility. This loving interaction and positive example is of more value than many men ever realized. Ephesians 6:4 gives instructions for fathers to not provoke their children to wrath. This verse does not mean that a father will never annoy his children or that he should not correct them. It is impossible to teach without offering at least some correction!

Barnes' Notes on the Whole Bible offers this explanation of the phrase "do not provoke your children to wrath":

"That is, by unreasonable commands; by needless severity; by the manifestation of anger. So govern them, and so punish them—if punishment is necessary—that they shall not lose their confidence in you, but shall love you. The apostle here has hit on the very danger to which parents are most exposed in the government of their children. It is that of souring their temper; of making them feel that the parent is under the influence of anger, and that it is right for them to be so too."

While parents do have and should maintain authority over their children, the way they should deal with their children is with tenderness and understanding. This echoes the tender understanding authority that Christ showed His disciples and with which He deals with us.

YOU ARE THE PROVIDER OF YOUR FAMILY

It is also important to note that a father should take the lead in providing physically for his family (I Timothy 5:8). Allowances must be made in cases where age and physical health may limit what some men can do. However, to the best of his ability, a father is enjoined by God to do all he can to make sure his family has the basic necessities of life: food, clothing and shelter.

Most families in the Western world have far more than just the basic necessities, and that is laudable in most cases. The scriptural injunction is that fathers provide for their families' needs, but we understand it will likely not include all of their wants.

In the physical household, there will only be one "head" of a physical family, and God has decreed that to be the husband and father. However, other members of the family can fulfil various duties to serve the family and see that the needs of the household are met. God's intent is for all to work together in harmony and unity for the good of the family, although there can be only one "head."

YOU ARE CALLED FOR HONOUR AND RESPONSIBILITY

God has given the man a unique and special role in the family. His function in the family is to reflect that of Jesus Christ Himself. He is charged with nurturing and caring for every member of his family - of having that same tenderness and loving authority that Christ has for His Church. What a tremendous honour and responsibility it is to have the role of father and husband!

"By the time a man realizes that maybe his father was right, he usually has a son who thinks he's wrong."

- CHARLES WADSWORTH

REFLECTIONS

- What is the proper role of men in the family and society?

- What one or two things can you contribute to your community or neighbourhood?

CHAPTER 12

ENHANCE THE ROMANCE IN YOUR MARRIAGE

"Couples who know how to play and have fun together develop a bonding that can carry them through the most difficult of times..."

- **DR. STEVE STEPHENS**

DO YOU FEEL LATELY that, your marriage is missing something? Maybe you need a little more fun! King Solomon, the wisest man who ever lived knew the value of fun, he therefore advised husbands in the Book of Ecclesiastes that: "Enjoy life with your wife...". Similarly, today's couples need to make time to enjoy each other and revive the pleasure that the relationship is meant to generate. In his book, *Blueprints for a Solid Marriage*, Dr. Steve Stephens stresses that:

"Couples who know how to play and have fun together develop a bonding that can carry them through the most difficult of times...Yet most couples work too hard to really enjoy their life together, they feel that if they aren't doing something useful, they are wasting time." How true! He therefore offers good suggestions as to how to add more fun to your relationship.

Let us examine a few of them now:

MAKE TIME FOR FUN

With the hectic schedules that families have today, you need to remember to schedule time for fun. Declare one night of the week *"date night,"* or carve out sometime during the weekend to relax with your spouse. Mark it on your calendar, and protect that time slot. "If you wait until it's simple or convenient, you might have to wait a long time," writes Dr. Stephens.

USE VARIETY TO SPICE THINGS UP

Dr. Stephens reveals that: "When people get older and when they've been married longer, they just become boring…It's not that they mean to get boring, it's just that they haven't intentionally figured out what would be something fun to do."

So how can you avoid relationship boredom? Try something new together! In the book, Dr. Stephens tells us that he and his wife take turns choosing what activity they will do on their date. When it is her turn to choose, he must do whatever she suggests. The next time they go out, he chooses the activity.

He stresses: "Therefore we try brand new things that we never would have tried before, and the rule is that we can't complain. We have to do it and have fun,". So try something new, it can be an adventure that bonds you both together as a couple. And you may discover a fun activity that you would have never thought you would enjoy!

SPEND TIME WITH OTHER COUPLES

Often, the friendships that spouses bring into the marriage are the relationships they have had with their single friends. Although there is nothing wrong with this, Stephens says, single friends often don't share your "marriage" mentality or interests. They could inadvertently pull you away from your spouse rather than encourage the relationship.

He writes further: "If you find another couple that you can both click with, then you can go out and you can do these fun things together. What you are doing is supporting and encouraging the marriage," One of the best places to look for couples to hang out with, he says, is at your church. It can be awkward to be the first ones to initiate the relationship, but it doesn't need to be difficult. Suggest to the couple that they join you one night for dinner or for a movie. "There are a lot of couples out there that are just waiting to be asked," Stephens says.

LOAN OUT THE KIDS (JUST FOR A LITTLE WHILE)

Another advantage of developing friendships with other couples, especially if you both have kids, is that when you and your spouse do want a night alone, you can turn to your friends for your babysitting needs. Then, when they want a night out, you can offer to do the same for them. Perhaps the kids would also enjoy a night away from mom and dad! Try it!

INCLUDE THE KIDS (SOMETIMES)

Having fun can also be a family affair. A lot of couples think because they have kids, they cannot go out and enjoy themselves like they may have when they were first married. Here Dr. Stephens advises:

"When you add a couple more kids to the family, it really isn't that much more work…Often, the kids will amuse each other, and it actually makes it easier. It's not as romantic but you can say, 'Hey, we are all going to go out and do this as a family.'"

Load the kids up for a day at the park, or take them out for a picnic lunch. Have a game night at home, or watch a movie together. "A lot of times we use kids as the excuse," Stephens says, "but if you are creative, there are a lot of things you can do."

DO CHORES TOGETHER

Even housework and yard work can be fun if you tackle it as a couple. Whether it is cooking a meal, washing dishes, or working in the garden, doing the job with your spouse can make it less mundane. "You can chat while you are doing this," Stephens says. "You can have fun. It gets done a lot faster, and it's not as boring."

Working on household chores together also helps couples resist resentment that can sometimes build up if one person feels they do more work around the house than the other one does. "If you are both working at the same time...if you work together and then play together, then there's no resentment" counsels Dr. Stephens.

FUN DOESN'T HAVE BE EXPENSIVE

Many couples think they can't afford to have fun, but they don't have to spend a lot of money to enjoy time together. Anything can be fun... "One of the easiest things to do is to say we're going to get a DVD tonight, and then we are going to fix some popcorn and cuddle up on the couch to have an in-house date." Stephens suggests.

In *Blueprints for a Solid Marriage*, he offers other affordable ideas that can help you tremendously:

- *Take in a sunset.*
- *Learn a new card game together.*
- *Listen to your favourite CD.*
- *Dance in your living room.*
- *Play charades.*
- *Play hide-and-seek.*
- *Share scary stories.*
- *Sleep in the backyard.*
- *Talk in rhyme for one hour.*
- *Walk in the moonlight.*
- *Write a romantic poem together.*

LET THE FUN BEGIN! Whatever activity you choose, keep in mind that the main objective is to have fun. Resist the temptation to fill the time with conversation about work, bills, or to-do lists. Use the time to enjoy your spouse. Remember, this time is just as important as anything else you do for your family. Start today and play your way to a healthier and happier marriage. You can do it! IT works! Try it from today![16]

---

[16] Reference: © 2016 The Christian Broadcasting Network, Inc., A non-profit 501 (c) (3) Charitable Organization.

REFLECTIONS

- How will you keep the flame burning in your marriage?
- List some activities that you will adopt and consistently practice towards your spouse
- Be spontaneous!

CHAPTER 13

DEALING WITH TEMPTATIONS THAT ENTRAP MEN

"You can't keep the birds from flying over your head,
but you can prevent them from building a nest in your hair."

- MARTIN LUTHER

TEMPTATION IS A CONDITION that is common to every human being. Even our Lord Jesus was tempted. In fact, His grew more and more intense than all other human beings combined, but He was able to overcome them all. And He was a man! Temptation is real, but know that temptation is not sin. It is a luring moment to draw you out of the will of God, but you can resist it and flee from temptations. That is what Martin Luther meant when he said concerning temptation, "You can't keep the birds from flying over your head, but you can prevent them from building a nest in your hair." Men face temptations, but we can overcome them!

The Lord Jesus Christ taught us to pray that God would not lead us into temptation, but this should not be interpreted as meaning that we will never be tempted. We will. And we are, every day of our lives. Whenever we find ourselves in temptation as men, we have a choice to make. We can either remain loyal to God and our integrity, or we can rebel, fulfil our lusts and so, worship the flesh and indirectly, the devil!

At the point of temptation, one of two things can happen: either we will *fall through* the temptation into sin. Or we will *grow through* temptation into greater levels of sanctification in the Lord and in life. Either of these represents a change point. The objective for every Christian man ought to be to make the most of every temptation for advancing our walk with the Lord.

AS MEN, we want to be the kind of men our families, children, colleagues and friends can respect and trust. But that can feel like the tallest of orders when the way you want to be seen on the outside seems so far removed from the way you feel on the inside. If good men are confident, capable winners, the compulsion to mask your insecurities and fears can feel impossible to resist. Unfortunately, the very temptations we entertain for the sake of strengthening our perceived manhood only serves as the most dangerous of distractions.

As men and as fathers, we want temptation to be a positive, not a negative, change point in our lives. But for this to be the case, we need to master our affections and be disciplined. Before we can live a life of moral discipline, we must first face the reality of temptations that are peculiar to men. To help us, I have chosen Dr. Gregory Jantz's book titled, *Battles Men Face: Strategies to Win the War Within* as case study for us. This book focuses on men and their anxiety triggers and addictions. In that book, he outlined some key areas that men are easily entrapped and easily tempted. I will touch on a few of them below.

MEN AND TEMPTATION

Giving in to a temptation can fill a void, but only in the short term. This sets the stage for chronic compulsions, entrapping good men in a vicious cycle of destructive behaviour. Here are the five most common temptations that entrap good men:

1) WORK

Few activities fulfil so many inherent needs among men as our work. As providers and protectors of our families, work is the means by which we maintain financial and physical security.

As natural competitors, work presents a practical, productive means of *"winning"* with every milestone of success. As members of our communities, work is a status symbol, informing our place on the totem pole, so to speak. For all of these reasons, the temptation is great for us to tip the scales of life in work's favour. As a result, the very behaviour intended to make your family feel secure leaves them feeling abandoned.

Relationships with friends and neighbours may wane, too. Working every waking hour may earn you wealth, raises and promotions, but it earns you little in the way of genuine security for, and respect from, the people you should be working for i.e. your family and yourself included.

2) COMPETITION

Though already mentioned as a factor in compulsive work habits, competition among men is worthy of attention all its own.
Men are competitive by nature. It's in our DNA, ensuring from the earliest of times that we will fight for the survival of ourselves and those we love. Of course, in today's society, the stakes rarely escalate to *life-or-death* situations.

Yet that competitive nature remains, compelling us to work and play hard for reasons beyond earning a living and having fun with family and friends. Winning — on the job, on the field or even in an argument with a family member or friend — feels good. It's like a drug, producing the kind of "high" that says you're good enough. In fact, you're the best!

Of course, it's the ego we're talking about here, meaning it feeds on the empty calories of competitive compulsive behaviour. Any dominance you feel from winning is nothing more than illusion. Once the game is won, the illusion crumbles, creating the need for yet another competition to fill the unquenchable void.

3) SEX

Of all the expectations made of men from *the most primitive* of times, procreation tops the list. Unfortunately, in this day and age, we are tempted to fulfil our high sex drives in ways that can do more harm than good. At its height, sex is an act of pleasure shared by two people engaged in an intimate relationship — connected *physically, emotionally, mentally* and *spiritually.*

Unfortunately, sex also exists as a pursuit in and of itself. Sex not only provides for the physical pleasure male bodies naturally crave, but it also boosts the ego for men who associate sex with their very sense of self. The bottom-line is, the more sex you have emotionally disconnected from your sexual partners; the harder it will be to reconnect with true intimacy in future relationships.

4) PORNOGRAPHY

In the pursuit of satisfying our sexual desires, men are increasingly turning to the "*sure thing*" of pornography. Pornography uniquely appeals to the visually sensitive nature of men, and the more graphic, the better. That is why it is a progressive compulsion, meaning we need increasingly crude, corrupted depictions of sexual acts to ensure continual stimulation.

The more we view, the more desensitized we become. In turn, many men find themselves turned on by sexual acts that once may have elicited feelings of disgust. In other words, pornography - sought out as a means of pleasure and or escape - often ends up imprisoning men in a world of guilt, shame and pain.

5) DECEPTION

Inherent in the compulsions that entrap good men is the temptation to use deception as a means of control. With clients, you fudge the facts to land the deal. With family, you make promises you know you can't keep. With sexual partners, you say things you don't mean.

Yet all this deception aimed at controlling your compulsions inevitably ends up controlling you. The anxiety associated with maintaining a false perception further bankrupts the pleasure you so desperately seek.

BEWARE OF 'THE SAMSON SYNDROME'[17]

SAMSON WAS CHOSEN BY GOD, and given the call to deliver God's chosen people. Samson could not succeed in that mission because of his own ego in the way. Mark Atteberry breaks down the book into twelve tendencies for the present day man. Each tendency is broken down into a chapter and backed with scriptural reference. Also each tendency is given a

---

[17]*The Samson Syndrome*: What You Can Learn From the Baddest Boy in the Bible by Mark Atteberry.

familiar story of those strong men in your lives (including yourself).

The Samson Syndrome offers readers powerful ideas for making sure they use their greatest strengths to honour God in every situation. A few of the tendencies discussed include:

- *Strong Men Tend to Disregard Boundaries*
- *Strong Men Tend to Struggle with Lust*
- *Strong Men Tend to Ignore Good Advice*
- *Strong Men Tend to Use Anger as a Tool*
- *Strong Men Tend to Have Big Egos*
- *Strong Men Tend to Take Too Much for Granted*

I would recommend it to mostly young men, but women could also take some knowledge and wisdom from it. Pick up a copy because it is a worthwhile read and you won't be disappointed.

THE MAN SAMSON (JUDGES 16-21)

Before Samson was born, an angel of the Lord came to tell Samson's parents that they would have a son. This boy was to be set apart for the Lord. He would be raised as a *Nazirite*. This meant he could never eat or drink anything from the grapevine, he had to stay away from graves, and he could never cut his hair. This will be an important thing to remember this week.

As Samson grew up, the Spirit of God came upon him. Samson was very strong. God planned to use Samson to deliver the

Israelites from the power of the Philistines. Samson was determined to marry a certain Philistine woman. A foolish bet with her people turned into several battles in which Samson killed many Philistines. Samson's life was full of pride, anger, and violence.

HERE COMES DELILAH (JUDGES 16:4-21)

Samson was a leader of the Israelites, even though the Philistines still ruled over them. Samson had a reputation as an extremely strong and fierce enemy of the Philistines. The Philistines continually looked for a way to trap him (Judges 16:2). Samson fell in love with another Philistine woman. Her name was Delilah.

"The rulers of the Philistines went to her. They said, "See if you can get him to tell you the secret of why he's so strong. Find out how we can overpower him. Then we can tie him up. We can bring him under our control. Each of us will give you 28 pounds of silver."

- **JUDGES 16:5**

So Delilah asked Samson to tell her the secret of his great strength. This would seem like a great opportunity to give God the praise for the strength given to him. But instead, Samson lied to Delilah. He told her that if someone tied him up with seven leather straps that were not completely dry, then he would become as weak as any other man.

So, the Philistine rulers gave Delilah the seven leather straps. Hold up your leather strips. Then the men hid in the room while Delilah tied up Samson. We are not told if Samson was asleep, or if he allowed Delilah to tie him up, the way a father might allow his young child to tie him up, knowing he could easily escape. After Samson was tied up, Delilah shouted to him.

"She said, "Samson! The Philistines are attacking you!" But he snapped the leather straps easily. They were like pieces of string that had come too close to a flame. So the secret of why he was so strong wasn't discovered."

- **JUDGES 16:9b**

Delilah told Samson that he made her look foolish by lying to her. Again, she pleaded for Samson to tell her how he could be tied up. Samson must have thought it was all a joke. This time he told her that if he were tied up with ropes that had never been used, he would become as weak as any other man. Hold up your ropes.

So Delilah got some new ropes and tied Samson up with them. Just as before, men were hiding in the room. Again Delilah shouted that the Philistines were attacking. Samson snapped through the ropes as if they were threads. Drop your ropes.

Once again, Delilah told Samson he was making her look foolish. Again, she begged for an answer to her question of how to tie him up. Remember that Samson's hair had never been cut. He wore his hair in seven braids. This time, Samson told her that if she were to weave the braids of his hair into the cloth that was on her weaving loom, he would become weak. Hold up your cloth.

Delilah waited until Samson was asleep, then she took the seven braids of his hair and wove them into the cloth on her loom. Once more, Delilah shouted that the Philistines were attacking. Samson woke up and broke free with no problem. Drop your cloth.

"Then she said to him, "How can you say, 'I love you'? You won't even share your secret with me. This is the third time you have made me look foolish. And you still haven't told me the secret of why you are so strong." She continued to pester him day after day. She nagged him until he was sick and tired of it."

- JUDGES 16:15-16

Finally, Delilah wore Samson down with her nagging. Samson was so annoyed by her repeated words; he couldn't take it anymore.

"So he told her everything. "I've never used a razor on my head," he said. "I've never cut my hair. That's because I've been a Nazirite since the day I was born. A Nazirite is set apart to God. If you shave my head, I won't be strong anymore. I'll become as weak as any other man."

- JUDGES 16:17

Delilah sent word to the Philistine rulers to come back one more time. They came, and brought the silver with them. Delilah lulled Samson to sleep. She called for a man to come and cut off the braids of his hair. Hold up your scissors and make the cutting motion. His strength left him.

Then, one final time, Delilah shouted to Samson that the Philistines were attacking. As Samson woke up, he thought he would break free as he always had before. Listen to what the Bible says next: **"But he didn't know that the Lord had left him." (Judges 16:20**). The Philistines grabbed him and poked his eyes out. They took him to Gaza, put chains on him, and put him in prison. Then Samson, once the strongest warrior in the land, spent his days grinding grain in prison.

We see that Samson did not inquire of God which woman he should pursue. We should always go to God first, and ask for His wisdom (Psalm 73:24, James 1:5). Samson did not take his parent's advice on this matter, either. The Bible tells us to ask the advice of godly people when we make decisions (Proverbs 15:22). We can read God's plan for choosing a wife in His Word. The Bible has wonderful guidelines for what type of woman makes a good wife.

For instance, it tells us that the most important thing is not her beauty, which will fade away, but that she loves the Lord (Proverbs 31:30). God's word also says not to marry a woman who nags or argues (Proverbs 19:13).

Other qualities to look for are a woman who works hard and helps those in need (Proverbs 31:17, 20). None of these qualities fit the women that Samson chose. Samson would have done well to seek godly wisdom about whom he spent his time with.

We should also seek God's wisdom about the people we spend time with. We should choose our close friends using the Bible as our guide.

For example, the Bible says not to spend time with people who get angry easily or those who gossip (Proverbs 22:24, Proverbs 16:28). Use God's wisdom to choose your close friends, because they are who you spend the most time with, and who will influence you. Also, listen to your parent's advice about who to have for a close friend. The Bible *promises* that things will go well for you if you honour parents (Ephesians 6:1-3).

Your parents can help you choose the type of person you should or should not have for a close friend. Now, we are not supposed to just ignore the other people in the world. They need to see our example. They need the Lord (Acts 1:8). Spend some time with them, but keep in mind that they are people that you are trying to help. Look for ways to tell them about God and His word. Do not allow them to influence you.

DELILAH'S FINAL PLEA TO SAMSON:

She said, *"If you love me, you will tell me your secret."* This is never a good sign! This is *manipulation.* That means, she was tricking him with her words. This situation had nothing to do with love! Delilah wanted the information so she would get paid with 28 pounds of silver.

She wanted to make Samson feel bad so that she could get what she wanted. Be very cautious of anyone who has similar words to you. If someone says, "If you are my friend, you will do this," or, "I won't be your friend unless you do this," watch out! (Proverbs 12:26). They are not trying to do what is best for you. They simply want something from you and they are trying to trick you. There should be no "conditions" on friendship (Matthew 22:39).

SAMSON'S DEATH: (JUDGES 16:22-31)

While Samson was in prison, **his hair began to grow again**. One day the rulers of the Philistines held a big celebration. They were going to offer a sacrifice to their false god. They believed their god had delivered Samson into their hands. Of course, this was not true. The Philistines were only able to capture Samson because the one true God left Samson when he treated the gifts God gave him so carelessly. During their celebration, the crowd called for Samson to be brought out. They thought it was funny to see Samson blind and weak. They wanted him to put on a show for them.

Samson asked the servant who was holding his hand to take him near the great pillars that held up the temple so he could lean on them. The Bible tells us that the temple was packed full of people. There were 3000 Philistine men and women on the roof of the temple in addition to all the Philistine leaders.

"Then (Samson) prayed to the Lord. He said, "Lord and King, show me that you still have concern for me. God, please make me strong just one more time. Let me pay the Philistines back for what they did to my two eyes. Let me do it with only one blow. Then Samson reached toward the two pillars that were in

the middle of the temple. They held the temple up. He put his right hand on one of them. He put his left hand on the other. He leaned hard against them. Samson said, "Let me die together with the Philistines!" Then he pushed with all his might. The temple came down on the rulers. It fell on all of the people who were in it. So Samson killed many more Philistines when he died than he did while he lived."

- JUDGES 16:28-30

Notice that Samson prayed for strength to get revenge for his own eyes. He didn't ask for strength so he could give God glory, or even to set his fellow Israelites free from the Philistines. Even in his final hour, Samson was thinking only of himself. Samson died in the temple that day. Then Samson's brothers and relatives got his body and buried him.

Samson's story is really a tragic one. We cannot hold Samson up as a godly hero that we should try to be like. Many times in the Bible, we see that God can accomplish His plans, even through the sins of men. In Genesis, Joseph's jealous brothers sold him into slavery, but God used it to save an entire nation from starvation. With godly vision, Joseph told his brothers,

"You intended to harm me, but God intended it all for good. He brought me to this position so I could save the lives of many people."

- GENESIS 50:20

Other examples of God accomplishing His goals through the evil deeds of men are found in Exodus 10:1-2 and Acts 8:4. Psalm 33:11 says, **"The plans of the Lord stand firm forever.**

What He wants to do will last for all time." God even used the self-centeredness, pride, and rage of Samson to accomplish His goal of rescuing His people from the Philistines. But because of all of his shortcomings, Samson lived a troubled life and died a violent death. With all the gifts God had given him, we wonder what Samson's life would have been like if he had lived according to God's laws.

IN THE STORY OF SAMSON, we must focus on the heart of God. Once again, God had heard His people cry out for His help. Even though they had turned away from Him over and over again, God heard them and wanted to help them (Judges 10:16). The story of Samson is the story of God rescuing His unfaithful people from the cruel hand of their enemy. It is a story of God's mercy. The dictionary says mercy is, "The power of a judge to pardon someone from their punishment."

Mercy is taking away punishment that is deserved. The Israelites deserved to be under the power of the Philistines because they turned their backs on the One who protected them. But, in His abundant mercy, God came to their rescue. That is the God that we serve - a God full of mercy. A God like that deserves our praise!

Samson can be seen as a symbol of the Israelite people. Just like Samson, the Israelites had been chosen by God to be set apart, to be used by Him (Deuteronomy 7:6). Just like Samson, the Israelites did nothing to deserve their blessings from God (Deuteronomy 7:7).

And just like Samson, the Israelites squandered, or wasted, the gifts God had given them. They did not use their blessings to glorify God. Instead, both Samson and the Israelites did what was right in their own eyes, not in God's eyes (Judges 17:6).

AFTER THE STORY OF SAMSON, the Book of Judges continues to tell of more failures of the Israelites. We learn of more *idol worship* (Judges 17:3-5). We learn of Levite priests who were not performing the duties that God had given them to do. Instead they chose to sin (Judges 17:7-12, Judges 19). And we even learn of Israelite tribes going to war with other Israelite tribes (Judges 20). The people in the Book of Judges had fallen a long way from the Book of Joshua when the Israelites worked together and obeyed God. There is a phrase that is repeated several times in the Book of Judges (Judges 17:6, 18:1, 19:1, 21:25):

"In those days Israel didn't have a king. The people did anything they thought was right."

- **JUDGES 17:6**

Look at the phrase carefully: "They did anything they thought was right." The Israelites did whatever felt right to them. The Bible calls this, "Being wise in your own eyes." Proverbs 3:7 says, "Do not be wise in your own eyes. Have respect for the Lord and avoid evil. A man who is wise in his own eyes is worse off than a fool! The men of Israel were completely foolish to turn their backs on God and do things their way. David did the same, when he refused to go to war at a time he was needed most at the warfront. He chose to be at the wrong place and by that, he was tempted and he fell flat:

*"In the spring of the year, the time **when kings go out to battle**, David sent Joab, and his servants with him, and all Israel...But David remained at Jerusalem."*

- **II SAMUEL 11:1**

God knows everything. Psalm 90:2 makes it clear about God that: *"From the beginning to the end, **You are God.** "* As men, let us learn to submit unto God and seek His guidance in all we do, especially as we attain greater success and prosperity in our fields of profession and ministries. Let us be honest with ourselves and listen to counsel, and as we do, we shall avoid the Samson Syndrome!

FOUR (4) IMPORTANT DISCIPLINES TO DEAL WITH TEMPTATION

• **Recognizing Temptation**

Firstly, we need to recognize temptation whenever it presents itself. As men, let us note that had David been able to see that remaining in Jerusalem rather than going out to battle as he should be, was a temptation of self-indulgence and a failure of his stewardship; he might not have fallen through temptation into adultery and murder.

To avoid the David situation, we have to be able to see through it to the dark, smiling face on the other side, inviting us to worship something or someone other than the Lord. Temptation is a kind of warning sign notifying us that the possibility of sin lies just ahead. The better we are able to recognize sin, therefore, the more alert we will be to temptation's presence when it arises. The place to begin in being able to recognize sin is with the Law of God (Romans 7:7).

If, as Psalm 1 recommends that, we make daily meditation in the Law of God part of our disciplines in seeking the Lord. We will be in a much better position to recognize temptation whenever it arises. In one way or another, every temptation begins with, *"Yea, hath God said…?"* It is the voice of the tempter in our conscience, inviting us to "reconsider" our logic. He tries to play down on the principles of God by us trying to manipulate God for our own advantage. For this reason, every man must know God and delight in His Word. We will be in a much better position to tell Satan where to get off whenever he suddenly appears, or one of his tempting hooks in our path.

- **Reorient Your Focus**

Temptation can distract us from a true understanding of who we truly are, whom we serve, and what we are to be about. When it was time to go out to battle that fateful spring, David must have thought to himself, "You know, I'm a bit weary of all this continuous fighting and securing borders. I deserve a good rest, at least this season! I'm worth it, isn't it?" You see, temptation always tells us, "You can be like God! Make up your own mind. Do what's best for you. Others will just have to look out for themselves!"

Temptation shifts the focus of our devotion off God and His Word onto our own most base affections. Temptation covers your eyes from the truth and keeps your mind on fantasies and the pleasure aspect of sin. Temptation makes us lose sight (temporarily) of our purpose as men and our responsibilities as fathers. Temptation makes us think about what is here right now, forgetting about consequences, repercussions and effects of wrongdoing.

In Psalm 73, the moment Asaph realized he was being tempted to be disloyal to God, rather than try to hide from God and His Word, like Adam in the Eden Garden, he ran to Him, resorting to prayer and meditation to get his mind back into a proper focus and orientation. That is what real men must do: run to the Father of all fathers for help. It is only when we are able to keep the eye of our heart fixed the Master that we gain the strength to continue obeying Him and to deny the invitation to rebel and fall into sin.

- **Resist the devil**

One problem that happens when temptation arises is that we tend to listen to it and the possibilities it suggests. We consider the delights – which are fleeting, to be sure, though we do not dwell on that - which temptation volunteers. We turn the 'apple' of temptation over and around, sniff and squeeze it in our minds, imagine ourselves tasting it, and listen to every word of the devil as he says, "This will be cool. It's all right. Think about it this way." Soon enough, we are ensnared and on the way falling!

Jesus Christ typically had but a few words for the demons whenever He confronted them: *"Shut up! Get out!"* He silenced the devil without an argument simply by refocusing on the Word of God and reciting it aloud. James promises that if we resist the devil he will flee from us (James. 4:7). We can do this by seeking the Lord in prayer, calling to mind passages and teachings of God's Word that have a direct bearing on the temptation before us, and just telling the devil to bug off.

Do not try to skip this step. If you do, the only resources you will be likely to have on hand for resisting temptation will be those of your own wits and strength. And that would not get the job done. Resist the devil with the Word of God and the shield of faith expressed in prayer, and he will leave you alone soon enough!

- **Resume**

Finally, move on in your walk with the Lord. Do not linger around the crossroad of temptation. Keep going forward toward what is right. Wherever temptation is suggesting where you must go, head in the opposite direction. If you are considering something contrary to the Word of God, envision yourself doing something contrary to that. "Contraries are by contraries cured," explained the ancient Celts. Take the next step, and the next step to keep you moving along the path of righteousness and the way of peace and joy.

Temptation can be an important change point in your life, moving you along into greater heights of spiritual maturity in the Lord. But you need to attack it faithfully, diligently, and with a conscious and determined effort to grow through, rather than fall through, the temptations you will encounter each day.

Make a list of the temptations you might reasonably expect to encounter today. Then, prepare for each of these in a time of prayer and meditation. Take each one as it comes throughout the day. At the end of the day reflect on any ways temptation served as a change point in your life. Share this experience with a Christian friend.[18]

---

[18] Reference: *Renewal as a Way of Life: A Guidebook for Spiritual Growth,* by Richard Lovelace, You might also like to read *"The Nature and Nurture of the Soul,"* a free View Point study.

REFLECTIONS

- Carry out a self-assessment regarding safeguarding your marriage.

CHAPTER 14

MENTORING THE BOY WITHOUT A FATHER

"Being a father is the most important role I will ever play and if I don't do this well, no other thing I do really matters."

- MICHAEL JOSEPHSON

RAISING A BOY IS A VERY TOUGH JOB for any parent. So you can imagine that young boy, whose father is absent in his life, living with a single mother, who is struggling on her own to raise that boy into a young man. Without the father in the picture, you see the mum and son often facing a plethora of challenges unknown to the regular family.

Here we are looking at a single mum who must be the breadwinner, the role model, the teacher, the disciplinarian, the protector, and the provider for her child's training, education, health, and general welfare. That is scary, isn't it? Firstly, being a woman, she has no idea what it is really like to grow up as a young man and the psychology of a growing young man, who is transitioning from those boisterous years of early teens, through adolescence into young manhood.

This is the season of life where a boy turning into a teen faces identity crises and can show rebellion and a lot of energy that even a man finds it hard to understand and manage. That is a dilemma indeed for a single mum who herself is struggling with her own feminine issues, coupled with her loneliness and trying to survive without a man (husband) in her life.

Any single mum of a super-active little boy can tell you that it's no easy task! Although a mum can work near miracles to give her son everything he needs, she will and can obviously never be a father. Of course, being in a fatherless family does not mean that you are doomed. There are a number of things you can do to help your beloved son grow into a happy, fulfilled and confident young man. Let me share a few of those intervention steps with you now:

PROVIDE ROLE MODELS

Find a father-figure for your boy to look up to. This is vital and very important for the successful growth and maturity of your son as he grows into a young man. His biological father not being around is unfortunate, but do not let that make you bitter; rather see to it that you make life better for your son and one day he shall congratulate you for that very important step you took on his behalf.

Another very important point here: Psychologists believe that, boys and girls should be surrounded by both sexes. Ensure therefore that he is exposed to such environment. He must not be exclusively surrounded my males, neither should he be raised in a mainly female environment. These have serious psychological consequences. So ensure he has many male role models, including uncles, grandfathers, senior brothers or cousins, teachers, Sunday school teachers, and close friends. Of course, as a single mum, you will be the ultimate role model for your son!

Remember also that your attitudes, moods, and outlook can alter your child's outlook. It is therefore more important than ever for you deal with your personal frustrations and maintain a positive appearance and attitude, because he picks up those non-verbal side of you quicker than you can imagine. Do not insult his father to his hearing. Do all you can to remove any form of resentment and bitterness from your heart.

See your son as God's gift to you, and do not look at him with painful memories of how his irresponsible father treated you. God knows you can handle it, that is why He has given you this bundle of life: your son. There are many wonderful men who are holding key positions in high places of life, who were raised by single mothers. You can be one of such sweet mothers so be inspired to get all help and support you need to raise your son in the best way possible and God will help you achieve it!

MAKE TIME FOR YOURSELF. Do meditation and reflect on your life often, and show him the best of attitudes you can muster courage to show. If you are a Christian, attend church services with him and ensure he enrols in the Sunday School class that befits his age. Help him discover his talents and gifts and encourage him to serve in church and be active in his groups in the church. Do all you can to maintain an all-important balance in your life and the life of your dear son.

SET LIMITS

Many single parents try to compensate for the absence of a father by spoiling their child or by allowing their kids to do whatever seems good in their own eyes – they are allowed to 'rule the roost.' It is vital to note that, kids are kids and are like cement and sand: they need structure, moulding and limits. Teach your son the rules of the home and the expectations you have set for him.

Let him understand the reward-discipline system in place for him. Let him understand the consequences for poor behaviour. As well as rewards that go with good behaviour and encourage him to aspire for more rewards. Be consistent to teach him to live responsibly, respect others, especially elders, and show consideration for others.

Children *can* be raised successfully without a two-parent household; I can guarantee you that! It is all about how you set up your family. The kind of home atmosphere you create determines whether your child will succeed or fail in his future endeavours. I encourage you to create the best home you can ever think of.

ARRANGE FAMILY TIME

When young boys belong to a one-parent household, especially when mum is the primary caregiver, it is essential for you, the single mum, to spend quality time with your son. Kids are not demanding with what activities you do together, as long as you are giving him the *one-on-one attention* he thrives on.

Prioritize some quality time to read, play, watch television or movie together or just sit and talk with him. Your son just wants to have fun. You can even play football with him! He will probably be delighted to see you play him and try to show you how skilful he is in football. Let him score more goals against you. He loves it and will have good laugh and so will you!

SHOW LOVE

Being a single parent, handling many responsibilities and chores in your household, it can be easy for you forget to tell your son how much you love him. You may feel exhausted, agitated, and sometimes burnt out. You may just want to sit down and have a good cry. That is okay, as it helps you ventilate pent up feelings. Despite all these, keep on providing unconditional love to your child and show him more affection.

Know that, young boys need more constant affirmations such as: praise, support, and a sense of security, especially when the father is absent. Clinical psychologists assert that, it is very important to try to see things from your son's perspective. Accept his emotions and regulate your own to provide him with everything he will need to be growing up a happy and positive-thinking child, with or without a dad. That helps develop a good character and a healthy personality, as he moves from boyhood towards adolescence and ultimately, manhood. That is a major key to unmaking authentic manhood!

REFLECTIONS

- In your community identify a young boy living with a lone or single parent.

CHAPTER 15

RAISING TOMORROW'S FATHERS TODAY

"Fifth Commandment: Honour thy father and thy mother: that thy days may be long upon the land, which the Lord thy God giveth thee."

- **EXODUS 20:12**
.

HAS YOUR FATHERING and mentoring methods for your own biological or foster family gone well? A man must be able to move further to offer mentoring opportunities at the work world. A good man is God's agent for transformation and change in the lives of others, especially younger ones. That is what mentoring is all about. *Father Matters,* a non-profit organization in USA has a programme called: *"Fathers Mentoring Fathers Program."*

The "Fathers Mentoring Fathers Program" is a five-session programme and covers five topics that are critical for today's active, effective, and involved fathers. It is a "men only" programme that provide a safe environment for the participants to open up their hearts and help one another work out their issues. Certificates are awarded upon completion. They have the following topics, which I recommend to men's groups here in Ghana and Africa to adopt:

- **COMMUNICATION**

This covers the importance of communication between *a father and his family*. Stressing how fathers have a significant impact on their children's learning and behaviour. How there comes a point in their lives when they must figure out who they are and how they must overcome the communication barriers that exist in order for their families to break free of the negative cycles that are blocking them from becoming a better person for their families.

- **TIME AND COMMITMENT**

This stresses that a relationship is based on *quality time.* In this session men learn that what they do speak louder than what they say and that they must use their time wisely to be good role models for their children. Ultimately they come to learn that if they do not take the time to influence their children, someone or something else will.

- **RESPONSIBILITY**

Here, the men discuss the need to *take family responsibility more seriously.* Men come into their role as a father when their child is born and learn how to address the different and complex aspects that come with fatherhood. Unfortunately, in today's world the family dynamic is growing more and more complex with the stresses of blended families, financially stressed homes and the involvement of significant others.

Men must understand how to navigate these challenges in a positive and healthy manner. In the session facilitators teach the men that fatherhood is no longer necessarily based on a biological bond, but rather on the social realities of today.

- **DUMPING THE GARBAGE**

In this session, men are reminded again that children will be apt to do what they do, not necessarily what they tell them to do. *Fathers must show active interest in the lives of their growing children.* For this reason, men cannot expect their children to lead moral and ethical lives if fathers themselves are not willing to identify and acknowledge their areas of need.

This session is dedicated to helping men take personal inventory of their character and behaviours and to commit to cleaning up these toxic behaviours that keep them from being the very best they can be for their families. Some of the areas discussed are:

- Alcoholism
- Adultery
- Drug Abuse
- Physical Abuse
- Mental Abuse
- Verbal Abuse
- Racism
- Inappropriate Sex

- **FUTURE FATHERS**

This last topic focuses on *the importance of joining and staying connected to a small men's group*. Women are very good when it comes to congregating to give each other emotional support. Men are different, and this is seen in most men's meetings or groups or fellowships. For this reason, we must make extra effort to gather as men, in small groups and talk about life, temptations and challenges that men face particularly.

Father Matters believes – and I also believe and advocate – that through such a positive action, men create an enabling environment – and even a therapeutic atmosphere – for themselves to deal with issues that only men can understand. Such small gatherings offer the opportunity for us to learn from each other and become participating fathers. Ultimately, we do not only become better men, but more importantly, our children will have better dads who are also mentors, coaches, counsellors and confidantes. That in my opinion is what we need today as men!

WHY WE NEED MENTORS

FATHER ABSENCE in many homes is among the most pervasive social problems challenging families today. But the presence of a *responsible father* improves a variety of outcomes for children and serves as a protective factor against problem behaviours including drug abuse, unwanted pregnancies, truancy, criminal activity, occultism among the youth, among many other factors. As a result, encouraging fathers to become more responsible, more available, and actively involved in lives of their children offers significant potential to empower individual lives, foster families, and contribute to the well-being of the community as a whole.

While the vision is to have all fathers positively involved in the lives of their children and families, mentoring or having the presence of a positive father-figure in the absence of a positively involved father has proven to be a very powerful tool for helping young people reach their full potential. Mentors and positive father-figures have what it takes to provide good support, advice, counsel, friendship, re-enforcement and role models.

QUALITY MENTORING RELATIONSHIPS offer significant potential to reduce the adverse effects of father absence by improving young people's attitudes toward parents, encouraging students to focus on their education, and helping children face daily challenges. Also, mentoring serves as an important means to promote responsible fatherhood through supporting and encouraging caring adults to become actively involved in the lives of children and youth.

Together, responsible fatherhood and quality mentoring brings hope and help to young people, through the power of physical presence. Many wayward boys will become good boys when they have a male figure they look up to as a role model and a father. So dear dad, whether you are interested in becoming a mentor, or connecting your child to a mentoring programme, learning more about what it means to offer mentoring and how to connect to a trustworthy person or programme. That is the first and most important step to helping our young men unmask their manhood and identify their true self and nature as boy who are developing into a man.

HOW DO I FIND A MENTORING PROGRAMME?

Whether you are looking to become a mentor or find a mentoring programme for your child, it is important to do a little research to find out what is available so you can connect to the right programme for you. To become a mentor, one of the first steps is to know yourself, evaluate your knowledge and your experience on mentoring. If after the evaluation, you seem to have average or below-average insight into mentoring, learn more about what it means to mentor. You can enrol in programmes available here in Ghana and online. Learn all you need to know about mentoring and the role a mentor has in the life of their mentees or protégés. I have a number of such programmes available for young people.

WHY DO I NEED A MENTOR?

MENTORING IS the active presence of a caring adult offering care, support, advice, counselling, coaching, friendship, reinforcement and personal examples to a younger generation of people. A good mentor is the one who has proven to be a powerful tool for helping younger people fulfil their potential. Research results show that mentoring achieves the following:

- *Mentoring improves young people's attitudes towards their parents, siblings, relatives, peers, teachers and leaders.*
- *Mentoring encourages students and mentees to stay motivated and focused on their education, and provides a positive way for younger people to spend free time with mentors and leave valuable things money cannot buy.*
- *Mentoring helps younger people face daily life's challenges and offers opportunities for the youth to consider new career and business paths, and get the much-needed skills and knowledge that offers economic as well as moral benefits.*
- *Quality Mentoring offers significant potential to reduce the adverse effects of father absence and serves as an important tool to promote responsible fatherhood by supporting and encouraging caring adults to become actively involved in the lives of children and youth.*

With the above benefits in mind, it is clear that, children and families benefit greatly from both *engaged fathers* and *positive adults* as mentors. It is paramount that we continue to promote, emphasize and encourage both positive father involvement and mentoring to help ensure a child's well-being now and in the future.

REFLECTIONS

- List 5 steps to take in order to raise tomorrow's fathers today

- Why do you need a mentor for your sons and daughters?

- Is there are mentoring programme in your community?

CHAPTER 16

BECOMING A SUPER-GRANDFATHER

"A father's need to be right. A son's need to be independent. A father's acceptance of his son as a man can be as difficult as a son's acceptance that his father is just a man. A father's need to be mentor. A son's need to be thought of as an equal. All these things make it difficult for fathers and sons to really get past their role expectations and really get to know each other and accept each other as they really are. "

– MICHAEL JOSEPHSON

BOYS GROW INTO MEN and men soon become husbands, then fathers! I remember the first time I became a father. It was not that easy, holding that tiny bundle of life in my shaking arms, looking intently at her face and wondering: "So I am a father now?" If you have been for many years now with kids, I am sure you will understand with me, how it means to be a parent and for that matter, a father or mother! I am not yet a grandfather, but I know that sooner or later, I will join the super granddad bandwagon. Therefore, this chapter is about the mastering of what I call post-fathering. Becoming a grandfather and what you need to know and to do.

As I began working on this book, I have been reflecting more and more on the things I have done well as a father, and the things I could have done better to become a really "super dad" for my wonderful children. Now I move farther into the future and begin to think deeply about becoming a grandfather, how does it look like? From the studies I have done and interviewing real grandfathers, I know that the transition from fatherhood to grand-fatherhood can be either quite exciting but perhaps more difficult.

As children come into a family after the parents are married and stable, learning about impending grandchildren can be quite a joyful experience. But guess when a child is coming unplanned, perhaps to an unwed teenage daughter. It can be a time of great stress and emotional pain. But, in any case, an innocent child is coming into a man's family, and despite the circumstances, there is a new opportunity to be involved in the life of this new little baby.

Grandfathers play such an important role in the lives of their grandchildren, from the earliest days of their lives through their growing up years. But some of the choices a grandfather makes can determine how successful he will be in this new and important part of his life. To help us appreciate very well, the art of mastering post-fathering life, I read much from an article written by Wayne Parker online and I share some of the key things he published, in paraphrased format. He offers seven tips that can help a father blossom in his role as a grandfather, and learn how to best influence little grandchildren for good and have fun in the process.

SEVEN WAYS OF BECOMING A GREAT GRANDDAD

#1: SPEND TIME WHEN POSSIBLE. There is no substitute for time in building relationships, and spending time with grandchildren is critical in that relationship as well. If grandchildren are far away, spending time can be on the phone, via web conference or in exchanging letters, texts or emails. If they are close by, then look for opportunities to see and spend time with the grandchildren often.

Being too intrusive in the lives of your grandchild's family can be a negative, so you want to be cautious. But make the time to see them regularly and to interact in positive ways. Even if the grandchildren tend to test your patience, make time to be with them and to get to know them well.

#2: RESPECT THE GRANDCHILD'S PARENTS. Meddling parents or in-laws can be the bane of a young person's existence, and that is never truer than when the kids are new parents. As the parent of a parent, you step into a different role – one of giving advice rather than directing outcomes.

So, as a grandfather, you need to respect the grandchild's parents and honour their wishes. You can certainly offer advice and counsel when you see things going awry, but you can't change discipline techniques or counteract their parenting philosophy. But you can always show love and make sure that your grandchildren feel close to you.

#3: PREPARE YOUR HOME. If grandchildren are going to spend any time in your home, you may need to take a critical look and baby proof your home. Put delicate things out of reach. Get a portable baby gate for the top of your stairs. Put child locks on cabinets and closet doors. If you can get your home ready to take care of grandkids, you will not spend all of your time telling them "no" and keeping them out of things.

#4: SPOIL THEM BUT CAREFULLY. Every grandfather looks forward to the opportunity to spoil his grandchildren and to give them things and time that will help them be happy. But grandfathers need to be a little careful as well. Feeding them ice cream half an hour before dinner is not a good idea.

Remember to think about the bigger picture when you are tempted to spoil them. It is also good to remember that kids love quality time spent with them as much or more than they love toys, video games and treats. Think more about making memories than adding to the toy box.

#5: FOCUS ON SIMPLE FUN. Sometimes, grandparents can be complicated as far as their interactions with the grandchildren. Try to keep interactions simple and direct. While a trip to Disneyland may be good occasionally, you don't have to have major league entertainment all the time. Reading together, playing with the kids in the yard and just talking over some treats can be the best interactions of all.

#6: GIVE AGE-APPROPRIATE GIFTS. Sometimes grandparents are so excited about giving gifts to the grandchildren that they forget what they are capable of enjoying. An electronic tablet might be good for a ten-year-old but not for a two-year-old. Think about their maturity level, their motor skills and their attention span when considering gifts for them.

And always remember safety for the smallest ones – too small parts can be choking hazards. Most toys have age guidelines printed on the box, and checking these are a good way to make sure that your gift will work and be a good thing for the kids.

#7: DON'T TAKE RISKS. Parents are often a little over-protective of their children, while grandparents have seen kids grow up with all kinds of risky experience and turn out just fine. But grandchildren are the not the ones with whom grandfathers should take risks.

Always buckle them up in the car in a safe car seat. If you take them on a motorbike, make sure they are wearing a helmet. Don't leave them out of sight anytime you are in charge. Just make sure that you are keeping the importance of their safety and health at the top of mind in your interactions.

Indeed, being a grandfather is a great work, mentoring the next generation today. Offering care and training to your grandchildren can be a lot of fun too, and of course, very rewarding if you follow just a few simple rules above, and take appropriate precautions, and make sure that you are having meaningful and fun interactions with the grandchildren.[19]

---

[19]Reference: Wayne Parker, *Seven Tips for Becoming a Super Grandfather*. © 2016 About.com - All rights reserved.

REFLECTIONS

- What does it take to be a great and a super grandparent?
- List 5 of the seven ways of becoming a great granddad
- What is your view of the concept of keeping aged fathers in Home for the Aged?
- Can we raise very successful children today, without the input of our fathers or grandfathers?

CHAPTER 17

STAYING CONNECTED TO GOD IN OLD AGE

"Older men are to be temperate, dignified, sensible, sound in faith, in love, in perseverance. Older women likewise are to be reverent in their behaviour, not malicious gossips not enslaved to much wine, teaching what is good."

- TITUS 2:2,3

IN THE BIBLE, APOSTLE PAUL was a spiritual father to many young men and women. In fact, he single-handedly discipled and mentored many young men, foremost among them being, Timothy and Titus. He established local churches in many cities and towns in the Asia Minor. On those churches he established, Paul ensured that he had pastor and bishops over the congregations. Obviously, the person he put in charge of those churches as pastors and bishops where those he had discipled, mentored and fathered, and they included Titus and Timothy.

Years later, he wrote a letter to Titus, whom he had made an overseer on some of the churches he established, he wrote a letter – an epistle – giving instructions on how to build a healthy church as well as the character attributes expected of a potential leader to possess. This is found in the New Testament book called the Book of Titus. Chapter 2 addresses the issue of the character of a healthy church, as well as what is expected of older men and women in the church:

"Older men are to be temperate, dignified, sensible, sound in faith, in love, in perseverance. Older women likewise are to be reverent in their behaviour, not malicious gossips not enslaved to much wine, teaching what is good."

- **TITUS 2:2,3**

For the purpose of this book, I want us to concentrate on the *older men,* and their conduct in the church, and the community, in general. I will delve deeper into the issue that Paul sought to address in this quote.

Let me tell you the truth that, today's society has the highest percentage of older people. This is especially very true of developed nations, such as the United Kingdom and the United States of America. For example, material comfort, medical care and a low birth rate have led America to what is called *the graying of America,* made up of an old population. In the USA, it is documented that, the number of people who over 65 years are far more than the number of teenagers. In fact, there are about 23 million teenagers in America, compared to about 35 million people who are over 65 years old!

This statistic then tells us that in 25 years from now, one out of every five people in the USA would be over 65 and one out of every ten will be over 80. That is 'the graying of America'! I do not have statistics for Africa, but I sense we may have a similar record. At least, we see it often – very unfortunately though – on obituaries here in Ghana that younger people are dying disproportionately, leaving their fathers and grandfathers living in misery.

As Bob Hope said humorously, "You know you're old when the candles cost more than the cake." Agatha Christie also wrote on one occasion that she married an archaeologist. And someone asked, "Why would you marry an archaeologist?" to which she replied, "Because the older I get the more he'll appreciate me!" That is humorous but you know, it is said that there are only three stages in life: *youth, adulthood*, and *"my, you're looking well."* Does that sound familiar? When people start saying that to you, *"my, you're looking well!"* Know where you are!

Now, there is the other side of the coin: the reality of getting older. That is not quite as humorous. I can testify to this as I turned fifty in 2016. Knowing that I am leaving behind youthfulness and embracing senility comes with certain sadness with it. Of course, fifty is still quite a youthful age – some call it *the childhood of old age!* When I stand in the mirror and look at myself with honest sincerity of assessment, I see the strings of grey hair and I know I am no longer growing younger!

You know, as we get older, we wish we still have youthfulness to express it. As someone said, "It's a shame that youth was wasted on people so young!" There are negative aspects to getting old, that is a fact. For example, we become creatures of formidable character, and we do have some unbreakable habits. The longer we live by certain habits, the harder they are to deal with. Even our besetting sins become so much a part of the fabric of our lives that we become blind to them and our conscience no longer screams at us. Sometimes we get a little bit obstinate and stubborn. Sometimes we think we know more than we actually do know.

Sometimes we think age equals wisdom, but we know too well that it does not! Of course, old age should bring wisdom, but it may not always do, because we fail to grow in wisdom that goes with the phases of our life cycle. That was why great and godly man like David ironically failed in his moral character during his midlife, as he was caught in midlife crisis. So was his son, the great and wisest king, Solomon. He was very spiritual during his youthful years and served God very well. Yet, during his old age, he drawn away from his God, and he was drawn away by his many foreign wives. That led him through the alleys of bad acts, which he later recorded and recounted in the Book of Ecclesiastes. I recommend that book to you, my dear reader. Especially if you are fifty years and above. Please read it and learn wisdom.

THANKS BE TO GOD, that both of them, David and Solomon – father and son – did not die without repenting and making amends with God. They had their intimate relationship with their God restored in their old age. They both repented and lived quality lives in their old age and died in the Lord. I am grateful and feel so good about that, as I wish all older men would do the same! We serve the God of second chance. He is always available to receive His children who become prodigal, but come back to their senses. Even in their old age, God is more than willing to forgive them and reconcile them to Himself, their Maker!

REMEMBER YOUR CREATOR IN THE DAYS OF YOUR YOUTH

THE BOOK OF ECCLESIASTES follows the Book of Proverbs in the Bible. In the final chapter – chapter 12 – Solomon offers some powerful insight for us all, especially those of us who have crossed beyond our fortieth into our fiftieth birthday and beyond. Once you have crossed thirty-five years of age, you have started on the journey down the side of aging, whether you agree to it or not! Solomon begins the final chapter of the book in this sober manner (verse 1);

> *"Remember also your Creator in the days of your youth. "*

Solomon counsels us: Enjoy God while you are still young. It pays to know God while you are young. Let God be the central figure in your life while you are young "before the evil days come." The implication is that, the older you get, the more the potential evil of life increases. Now, the word 'evil' in this context is not talking about evil as in wickedness or satanic acts, but he was talking about evil as in predicaments of life. He was referring to ageing process with its attended health issues in particular.

Solomon was stressing on the fact of life that, no matter how handsome you might be, ageing definitely eats away that facial look and make you look aged. No matter how agile you are, as you age, the fluids in your joints drain away and your movements slow down. You cannot do in sixty years, what you used to do so easily when you were thirty years of age. Those are the 'evil days' that comes in the life of every man on earth as he transits from youthful age to the old age. That is an undeniable fact of life, and the earlier you embraced it, the better your preparation to face the life of senility.

Ageing comes along with a certain feeling of fulfilment, especially as you look back and it dawns on you that you could have achieved ten times what you have achieved today. As you assess your life, you become gloomier and almost disillusioned about the life you have lived. Do not be deceived: this feeling does not come to only poor people; it dawns on even those who have achieved quite a remarkable and tangible wealth and worth in life. Ask all who are old – beyond the age 60 – and they will testify! Solomon calls those the years when you will say, "I have no delight in them."

When David got to that era of life, he of all men could not even feel or enjoy the company of a lovely woman! In his old age, the elders around him thought it wise to get a younger woman, a virgin to warm the body of David, but surprisingly, David could not feel anything for the young virgin and did not touch her all those months she tried to comfort him! That is the reality of evils days when you declare: *"I have no delight in them!"* Money. Sexual pleasure. High position. Prestige. Name them. You will one day lose delight in them all! It is therefore better you appreciate God now and make the best out of life NOW!

Live a quality life. Build a good name. Let your personal brand stand out to bless many. At the mention of your name, may your good name bring good smiles and good memories in many faces. Enjoy good and godly friendships. Mentor younger ones. Impart unto others what you have acquired over the years. Do not be selfish. Invest in others. Instead of stashing your wealth in banks, invest in your children's education and build quality lives, and you are on your way of leaving great inheritance and legacy for the next generation! Commit your life to God and enjoy God and make God the centre of everything while you are younger, before you will not be able to experience all the rich delights of His creation.

THE PICTURE OF OLD AGE

Solomon described old age as: "before the sun, the light, the moon, the stars are darkened and the clouds return after the rain…" There are *cloudy times* in life. Those are the more barren and bleak times in life when you are old, perhaps in your late 60s and into your 70s and 80s. Those are the era of life Solomon gets very prosaic, and describes poetically as:

"The day that the watchmen of the house tremble and mighty men stoop, the grinding ones stand idle because they are few, and those who look through windows grow dim; and the doors on the street are shut as the sound of the

grinding mill is low, and one will arise at the sound of the bird, and all the
daughters of song will sing softly."

Now, the picture is of a house above is symbolic of a human body. The watchmen of *the house*, some commentators feel, are the arms and the hands: those are the guards, the protectors, the defenders, and they start to shake as you get old. And *the mighty men* would be the legs, and they begin to stoop and bend. The *grinding ones*, the teeth, stand idle because they are few. The days Solomon wrote, there were no dental prosthesis such as false teeth and bridges and what have you.

Teeth do not work anymore, and those who look through windows grow dim, you do not see like you once could see. The *doors* on the street are shut as the sound of the grinding mill is low - could be the slowing down of some kind of internal processes. One arises at the sound of the bird. You don't need an alarm clock anymore. You wake up if there is a bird 50 yards away tweeting in a tree because you sleep so lightly.

As you age, you do not sleep as well as you used to when you were younger. All *the daughters of song* will sing softly. If you bring the whole women's cheer club together and all their high-pitched soprano voices sing in full glory, you feel nothing. Your sense of music appreciation is on all-time lowest point.

In verse 5, Solomon describes further that, men who once-upon-a-time not brave, fearless, courageous and were afraid of nothing, now become *"afraid of a high place."* Why? Because they are worried about their instability. They are worried they might fall and break some brittle bones. They are worried about the *"terrors on the road"* as they walk along. They fear of stumbling over a stone and fall and be severely injured.

Then *"the almond tree blossoms"* probably refers to the white blossoms on an almond tree, and means the hair grows white and hoary. *"The grasshopper drags himself along"* means the walk changes and the pace changes: you used to walk briskly and gallop your way up, but now, all of a sudden you are dragging and shuffling along the way. Eventually you reach the last moment of the evening and engulfed in total darkness, and the *"man goes to his eternal home."* Death lays its icy hands on you. Your days on earth are over!

Now your appointment on earth is over, and you have appointment with God: to face judgement on all that you did with the life, talents, time and other great resources your Maker gave you at birth. While on earth your funeral takes place and men gave wonderful tributes and wonderful accounts of the life you lived, and they mourn your loss, you are before your Creator. You face eternity, either in heaven or hell! Pause and think and meditate deeply on this. How old are you today? How long will you live? If you are to die today, what account are you going to give about your life to your Maker? Meditate on this now.

Solomon wrote in verse 6 that: *"the silver cord is broken"* maybe that refers to the spinal cord. Then *"the golden bowl"* – may be that means the brain and *"the pitcher by the well is shattered"* could very well mean the heart. *"The wheel at the cistern is crushed"* –that is the veins, the arteries and smaller blood vessels.

I am not fully sure of all the specific imagery I have employed here to interpret the ancient writings, but I see it as sort of the demise of a man in his old age and the dust returns to the earth, and as it was, and the spirit goes back to God! This is a bleak way to look at old age, but it is reality! All human beings face this process of life. If you have never experienced it – as I have not too – anticipate it for it is coming, sooner or later. Prepare for that day of appointment with death.

BUT THERE IS GOOD NEWS!

Just because you are growing old does not at all mean life is bleak. Are you a Christian? Is Christ in you? Then, **"Christ in you, the hope of glory!"** As a Christian, know for certainty that, there is a crown awaiting you in eternity. It does not matter how long you live – because it is not everyone who lives into old age. What counts most in eternity is what you do with your life as a Christian or God's child. Jesus Christ lived for only thirty-three and a half years on earth, yet He accomplished so greatly for our salvation that today, after 2000 years, at the mention of His name, many rejoices and bow in worship of the Father! So it is about how worthy you live, not how long or short you live on earth!

As a Christian, even here on earth, you will be rewarded for the good works you do for Christ's sake. When you live a purpose-driven life, you are celebrated right here when you are alive! Your life is crowned in your lifetime. Many applaud your level of spiritual maturity and seek to emulate you. Many seek your mentoring and fatherhood.

LOOK FORWARD TO OLD AGE POSITIVELY

ARE YOU IN CHRIST? Have you walked with Him for any length of time? Then you should look forward to old age with joy, because it takes you nearer to heaven! The thoughts of old age put us in a situation where we have accumulated spiritual experience, which makes us truly rich! It enables us to be the great fathers, leaders, mentors and role models and the examples the younger generation need desperately. It allows us to filter out our life and keep what we think is really valuable to impart unto others. Physical ageing should therefore should be a good time to impart wisdom and gifts unto the younger ones.

You know, in the life of the church community, it is really very important to have people who are godly senior citizens. That was what Paul was saying to Titus, his protégé. He was saying to him: "As you look at your congregation, Titus, you need to start your instruction with the older people because they are so crucial." There are a lot of churches today that are filled with young people, being led by relatively young leadership and pastors. That is good, but not good enough! Why do I say so?

I think that such churches would be a very difficult place to minister the truth about realities of life, because they all seem to be peers and have had no valuable experience in life. They have not travelled through time, so they speak more theories than a mixture of theories and life's practical experiences.

A church that has average age groups of forty and below might be highly charismatic and full of life and vivacity, but will lack a lot of maturity when it comes to realities of living a life. Many of the members might have not gone through certain temptations, tests and trials of life, and so they are bound to fall into deep traps, except they have good mentors and spiritual fathers who are more mature and have gone through life's stages – including midlife, pre-senility and senility.

As a church or organization, you need some people who have been where all the younger ones are going, who can help them evaluate what they think at this present time. The younger ones need mentors who have been through failures in fields the younger and more energetic ones are now speedily going through. They need mature people with scars to point them to potential dangers of fallings and failings ahead, to help them to avoid such mistakes and pitfalls.

WE NEED THE HOARY HEADS! We need the aged and the wise, who have come and gone and have been there before, to instruct the young, and to show them the path of righteousness. We need more old ones to show our youth the path of goodness, and to show them the proper priorities and values of life. We need some people who can stand with the Apostle Paul and declare triumphantly:

"I've fought the good fight; I've kept the faith."

So dear reader, the aging of Christians is a blessing and not a burden! Older believers should be in great numbers in the future in the Church. That will bring balance to the church, and make the church a better and a richer place. The maturity of godliness will be a great blessing to the Body of Christ. God Himself respect old age and has told us to revere those who are older than we are - those who are the aged, who have walked with Him:

> *"You shall rise up before the grey headed and honour the aged."*

> ### -   LEVITICUS 19:32

> *"Wisdom is with the aged...with long life is understanding."*

> ### -   JOB 12:12

Indeed, gray head is *a crown of glory* if it be found in the way of righteousness. Somebody old who has walked a long time in the path of righteousness is a treasure of wisdom and a treasure of experience and a fountain of understanding. He is a triumphant Christian who has fought the battle over and over and over and been victorious – like David! He has experienced everything that the young are waiting to experience. He is a great treasure to the church and must be cherished and celebrated.

In Psalm 71:17, the psalmist sung: *"O God, Thou hast taught me from my youth, and I still declare Thy wondrous deeds. And **even*** *when I am old and gray, O God, do not forsake me*, *until I declare Thy strength to this generation, and Thy power to all who are to come.*" David's heart cry was that, "God give me a ministry in my old age because I can talk about Your strength, and I can talk about Your power because I've seen it for so many years - I've lived it!"

In Psalm 92, a very similar prayer arose from the heart of the psalmist, starting there in verse 12, "*The righteous man will flourish like a palm tree, he will grow like a cedar in Lebanon. Planted in the house of the Lord, they will flourish in the courts of our God. They will still yield fruit in old age; they will be full of sap and very green, to declare that the Lord is upright.*" Those who can best declare the character of God are those who have walked with Him longest.

OLD AGE IS A BLESSING TO ALL WHO WALK IN RIGHTEOUSNESS. Older people must be celebrated in any society. Why? They are the real treasure and carriers of history and they are a tremendous blessing. They bring spiritual experience, spiritual strength, spiritual endurance, and spiritual wisdom to all of us. If in the years ahead the church has an abundance of such people – and they walk in the way of righteousness – that is a great source of blessing!

That was what Paul sought to communicate to Titus. There is no value in being old if you are not godly. There is no value in being old if you are not a role model or a good example for others to follow and emulate you. The Apostle Paul laid down some very specific characteristics that are to be manifest in the older people in the congregation. Let us look at some instructions he gave concerning the men.

WE NEED MORE PRESBUTĒS IN THE LOCAL CHURCH

PAUL WROTE: "*Older men are to be temperate, dignified, sensible, sound in faith, in love, in perseverance*" (Titus 2:2). Now "*older men*" as used in this context, is from an interesting Greek word, *presbutēs*. It is a word that means just that, "*older men.*" Paul for example, used it in Philemon, verse 9, when he refers to himself as "*Paul, the aged.*" Perhaps Paul was in his sixties to early seventies at that time. He was talking about a man at that point in his life, when he no longer has to produce biological children, but to mentor younger ones, raising foundations of future generations.

There are some ancient personalities, such as Philo and Hippocrates, who used the same term – *presbutēs* – to refer to people over fifty years of age. That means, somewhere in the fifty and over and sixty and over, are the category this term refers to. The Apostle Paul was an old man by this term, in his sixties, way beyond fifty. So we are looking at that generation of men in the life of any local church.

PRESBUTĒS ARE THE MEN, called to be spiritually responsible and to demonstrate godly character. This role was very important in the local church in the days of Paul that, if they did not fulfil this duty, they were rebuked. Back in I

Timothy 5, Paul instructed: *"Do not sharply rebuke an older man, but rather appeal to him as a father."*

Now the assumption here is that, in the life of a local church, older men are likely to go wrong or sin. And that is true because they are still human. But it does not mean that "because I'm older - I'm over fifty, over sixty, over seventy, or over eighty – so all of a sudden, I don't sin anymore!" that is a big fallacy.

It is very reasonable to assume that the very fact that Paul is telling Titus to tell these men to behave well, is an indication that there is a real possibility that some of them might fail morally. It is indicated in Paul's words in I Timothy 5:1 that elders (older men) may need to be rebuked. They may need to be confronted about their sin. Paul wrote: **"If you do it, don't do it sharply."** Or better put: **"Don't do it cruelly."** The word here, the verb here, is used only here, and it means *"to beat with blows,"* or *"to strike with a fist,"* and allegorically *"to abuse verbally,"* *"to hammer with words,"* one lexicon elucidates.

Thus, if you are going to rebuke *an older man,* you do not want to hit him, you do not want to strike him, you do not want to hammer him with unkind, abusive, violent, harsh words. The verb Paul used here is related to the Greek word *plēktēs.* He used in I Timothy 3, and it means *"a striker"* or *"a hitter."* You do not want to hit them and strike them and abuse them and be harsh with them.

Confronting an older man's sins or wrongdoing has to be done without violence and without harsh action. It must be done graciously, kindly and with decorum. In I Timothy 5:1, Paul wrote: "*Appeal to him as a father*" using the Greek word, *parakaleō*, which in context can be put this way: "come alongside and admonish and encourage and appeal to one." That means with the consideration and respect that you would give to your own father. That simply means, general regard for people in their senior years is of grave concern to God.

Indeed, God is very concerned about that because God reveres old age and fatherhood. That simply means, how you treat your father is a matter God is very much interested in. He even discussed it in the Ten Commandments. In fact, the death penalty was required for disrespect, for hitting, striking your father or mother, or for cursing your father or mother according to Exodus 21:15, 17. Those who are older are to be treated with kindness and love and with honour and respect. So when you confront an older man because of a sin he has committed, do it graciously and with discretion. You come alongside and appeal to him with the respect that you would give to a father.

NOW LET ME PUT A BALANCE HERE. The patriarchs or fathers are to be deeply respected, but it is required of them to also conduct themselves creditably and earn the respect. As older men in a church, they are to exhibit a life that is holy, godly and exemplary. It is required of them to become the mentors, role models for a level of godliness that must pervade the congregation, and influence the younger men and the women.

Now, Paul was saying to Titus, concerning older men who fail morally: *"You must confront the older men in your congregation and you must call them to this level of spiritual living, or else..."* The implication is clear: *"they must be so confronted."* Confront them in love with the intention to correct them and bring them back to order, and not necessarily to punish them. Leave the discipline aspect to God, who is the Father of all fathers.

So on one hand, lets respect our older generation, and on the other hand, let us hold them accountable for their behaviour – or misbehaviour – and accountable for their maturity and godliness. Every older man should set as his goal to come to the latter years of his life and be able to say with Paul, *"I have fought the good fight, I have finished the course, I have kept the faith"* (II Timothy 4:7). Every older man should be able to say, "I want you to be a follower of me as I am of Christ." Every older man should be able to say to the younger man, "**Let me show you how to live life.**"

Temperate:

As older men, we should have so much to offer. Paul suggests, first of all, three characteristics: *"temperate," "dignified,"* and *"sensible."* To be "temperate" literally means "not drunken." But figuratively it means *"moderate, not indulgent, not extravagant."* The older man is a man who is not into excesses. He must be generally a moderate person. He has learned the high cost of filling out all his pleasures, satisfying all his whims, and pursuing all his dreams. He is now filtered through all of that, and he is left a lot of stuff along the path discarded.

When he was younger, he poured out a lot of energy into a lot of things, but now that he is an older man, he can look back and see where that energy was wasted in so many cases. As a young man he dreamed a thousand dreams and wanted to accomplish a thousand things and looks back only to a handful of things that had eternal value. As an older man he has had a multitude of experiences, one after another, day after day, month after month, year after year, and life has been moderated by those experiences.

all the possessions and all the accumulation and all the reputation and all the achievement and all the accolades have been set aside on the path of life and discarded because they had no real value. He has come to a right value system, and like Solomon, he now declares: *"All is vanity…and meaningless!"* He has come to be, "**sober-minded**" as used in I Corinthians 15:34.

Another related word, used in I Peter is, "**sober in spirit.**" In other words, he has got his priorities right and he has put life in the right perspective. He now knows what experiences were valuable, and now he knows they rendered him the best of life's fruit. They made him the man he is today. In many cases what he did not want was what was most valuable, and what he pursued with all his might was least valuable! He knows that now and he has filtered the unprofitable habits out.

Now older man finds himself in the reality of life. He has therefore chosen to reduce life into a simpler lifestyle and simple living. He used to know many things, but now he knows only one thing and that one thing he knows is of eternal value. He now sees the real value of things. He has seen now that, relationships have real value, and is making efforts to invest more value into all his relationships – especially with the younger generation. That state is absolutely crucial for older to dispense to a younger generation.

It is like the father who sits with his little children and says, "I know you don't understand why. You'll have to trust me for this. You can't what you intend to do. I know why you can't do it. You don't understand why, but I've been there. I'll tell you why." That is what the Bible describes as sober-mindedness or sobriety. Another word for is its becoming temperate. We need more temperate men in the home, the society and in the church! Such men have their lives reduced to the irreducible minimums of what really matters in life!

Dignified:

Secondly, older men are to be *"dignified."* The Greek word for it is "semnos", which means: *"serious, worthy of respect, venerable."* It does not mean that they are boring and gloomy people. It just means they are no more frivolous or flippant. They are serious in life. They have lived long enough to see that life is a serious business and must be well-lived. They have gotten over that youthful exuberant life that makes young people feel they are untouchable, immortal and invincible!

Older men have seen too much and felt too much to be trivial! In most cases, they have buried their parents. They might have buried their sisters and brothers. They have stood in hospital's waiting rooms, while those they love died. They have been waiting for the surgeon to come out and explain what happened in the cancer surgery to a life partner. They have watched a teen-aged child rebel. They have watched a child born who turned away from everything they believed in and valued. They watched a child die of an incurable disease. They have seen it all and felt it all.

I am talking still about older men. They have borne the burdens of their own life and that of family as well as the burdens of a myriad of other people with whom they have shared life. They have seen their gargantuan dreams passed on, unfulfilled. They have been disillusioned before. They have experienced midlife crisis with its attended negative repercussions. They know for sure that, the world is not going to get any better, and they have little power to change the world. They have learned to allow God to be supreme and sovereign in His will in human affairs.

They have learned the sober truth that, no matter what, we are humans and cannot know it all. They have lived through the hopeful euphoria of youthful life that claimed, *"We're going to fix everything!"*. And they are down on the other side of life: reality. They know with all honesty, that life is the way it is because man is the way he is, and that, man is not going to change by himself, and that only God has the power to change lives and transform people!

Sensible:

Finally, Paul wrote that, the older men's lives should be characterized by what is *"sensible."* That means they should be *"sensible."* This means they must have *discretion* and *discernment*. These two attributes come by age. You can only learn to be sensible. It is not a gift that is given you; you live it and earn it. It is a life's experience.

They have gone through all the experiences of life, and they have developed strength of mind and a depth of experience and a grip on truth and a devotion to what is right. They have learned – through 'trial and error' – how to control their instincts and their passions, and balance it with God's Word and principles of life.

And that word *"sensible"* also means older men have got the loose ends of their life tied down. They are under control. They have discernment and discretion. They have "sound judgment" and they think soundly. They hardly act on impulse. They give room for a matter to breathe before they judge on it. That is maturity that comes not by charisma, but by character.

Thus, all the three qualities - being *temperate, dignified* and *sensible* – are the antidote for curing the 'disease' of the excesses of youthful exuberance, such as: recklessness, impulsiveness, thoughtlessness, rebelliousness and instability. Paul then sums up the three positive virtues in the final statement: *"sound in faith, in love, in perseverance."*

"SOUND" HERE MEANS "healthy, without weakness, without disease, without debilitation." They have strong, well, whole attitudes in these areas. First "in faith", means they are to be healthy in faith. They have spiritual faith that is healthy, whole, well, sound, and solid. What does that mean? That means their faith in God must be unwavering. They have seen enough in life and know a lot by experience – compared to the youth, who knows lot by theory.

The older man has been through enough in life. Having lived for 50, 60, 70, or 80 years on earth, they have seen a lot of how God works in man's affairs and can now trust God and advocate that God is to be trusted. They do not question God. They never lose their trust in God's good purpose and His intention. They never lose their confidence in God's plan for humanity. They never lose their hope for God's sovereignty.

They never accuse God of disappointing them. They never doubt the truth of the Scripture. They never question the power of the Holy Spirit at work among men. They never ever question whether the gospel can save. They know the effectual power of the Gospel, and they have experienced the power of God's salvation practically and personally.

Older men have lived through all the years God has blessed them with. They can testify of how God has shown Himself through all of the vicissitudes of life. They have seen the divine hand of God in their struggles and all the difficulties they have been through in life. They can testify that God has been there, and He has proven Himself, and they can declare with great confidence that: "**I believe God!**"

His faith is courageous because a life of believing has taught him to trust God. God has proven Himself faithful over and over the long years. Through all the temptations and the trials, the repentances and the renewals, and through all of the exposures to the Truth and the application of the Word, God has proved Himself to them. Their faith has matured and they demonstrate enough faith in the church, that younger ones can emulate their faith.

DO YOU FEEL SO OLD?

ARE YOU AN OLDER MAN? Are you above fifty years old? You are a powerful force in the church! Moses was eighty when God called him to lead Israel from slavery in Egypt! How old are you? Moses gave many excuses, but age was not one of them! So no matter your age, no not underestimate your character, capability and competence!

JOHN WESLEY, according to records, did greater works in his old age than his younger years in ministry. He travelled 250,000 miles by horseback or on foot to preach. He preached 40,000 sermons, produced 400 books, and understood 10 languages. One man's achievement! At eighty-three, he was annoyed that he could not write for more than fifteen hours a day without hurting his eyes! At eighty-six, he was ashamed that he could only preach twice a day! And he said at his eighty-sixth birthday that, he had to admit there was an increasing tendency to lie in bed until 5:30 am! How old are you today and what habits do you have?

MY DEAR FRIEND, you have so much to offer. You belong to a godly older generation, which the younger generation need desperately. It is crucial to the life of the Church. So spend the rest of your life giving back unto the younger ones, what God has helped you achieved today. In the words of Dr. Myles Munroe, **"DIE EMPTY!"** that means, pour yourself out unto others – especially your children and many others who look up to you. Write books for the future generation to read.

Speak into the lives of your children. Mentor more young people. Inspire the younger generation to do better than you did, building on the foundations you have laid. Ask God for grace and resources to complete your assignment on earth as a father and a mentor. At all cost, leave a lasting legacy that has your good name imprinted indelibly on it. When your name is mentioned, it must be a recounting of good testimonies about!

Make your good name be a reference point and make the memory of you live forever!

REFLECTIONS

- Spend some time to read through the Book of Ecclesiastes.

- Summarize the lessons you have learnt from Solomon in the Book of Ecclesiastes.

- If you have to teach your sons and grandsons 5 lesson from the Book of Ecclesiastes, what will they be?

Conclusion

FATHERS, LET US RAISE FOUNDATIONS OF GENERATIONS

"Great is the Lord, and greatly to be praised; and His greatness is unsearchable. One generation shall praise Thy works to another, and shall declare Thy mighty acts. I will speak of the glorious honour of Thy majesty, and of Thy wondrous works."

- **PSALM 145:3–5**

FROM ALL WE HAVE DELIBERATED ON this far in this book, it is no doubt that fathers play a vital and an essential role the building of the foundations of their children, and that whatever you pass on to their children by genetics and by their trainings go a long way to establishing a good ground for their children to build a successful life – or otherwise – in the future. This is more especially of the boy-child. It is expected of us as fathers, to be the best in anything we say and do.

As fathers, we are mandated to live according to the purpose of fathering: raising the next generation of children, who must be better than we have been. It is our mandate to serve as good examples, role models and mentors to children, who are the next generation, who are taking the fatherhood baton from us,

237

after our days are spend here on earth. That makes fatherhood a great privilege as well as the greatest responsibility of any man alive today!

Sadly, many fathers in our generation have lived outside their purpose and abused the raison d'être for living as men. They have imprinted very negative pictures on the minds of our younger generation. As the famous quote of Dr. Myles Munroe goes: *"When purpose is not known, abuse is inevitable."* Many fathers sadly have abused their fatherhood and therefore have unmasked young men who are also living outside their purpose. Go to our prisons and correctional homes: greater proportion of the numbers of the inmates are there directly because they had no responsible male-figure in their lives, especially during their childhood and or their teenage years. They had no man in their lives to help unmask their manhood in a proper way. This makes fatherhood so important.

Recently, I paid a visit to a correctional institute for teens in Accra with an organization that I serve as a mentor in. We had a wonderful time interacting with the young boys. Later as I reflected over the time I had with the inmates, sadly, a lot of them lacked good fathers, and most of them did not even have any father at home. Either their fathers refused paternity or that, they were present, but were very bad examples to their kids. That is, it.

A FATHER PRODUCES AFTER HIS KIND, most often than not! Indeed, everything rises and falls on fatherhood. It takes good fathers to make good homes. It takes good fathers to establish good communities. Without good and godly fathers, no nation can rise up in righteousness – the act of a society doing good and ruling and being ruled by right leaders, right laws and right attitudes of citizens.

I can therefore safely claim that, what every community and nation need first and foremost, is good fathers. When a nation is ruled by leaders who are good fathers at home, that nation is more likely to have good and great leaders who would guide the nation by righteousness, as the Good Book declares:

"Righteousness exalts a nation, but sin is a reproach to any people."

- **PROVERBS 14:34, NASB**

It takes righteous fathers to produce righteous leaders, and righteous leaders produce after their kind: a righteous nation that God exalts! What does a righteous father do? Righteous fathers spend quality time to teach their children how to respond positively to life. A righteous father is a godly man and seeks first to build a firm foundation for his children's lives. They are more concerned about their children's faith. A godly father invests time, instruction, love, and discipline in his children. He shapes the next generation and equips his children to share the concepts of Biblical living with future generations.

A GODLY FATHER IS the man who seeks after God and walks in God's principles for effective and successful living. He is a man of honour. His ways has much to be emulated and to look forward to. He is kind to children. He cares for children – not only his biological children. A godly father has deep compassion and sees to it that no child goes hungry or naked. He is more concerned about the building of the character and attitudes of children. He mentors many children. He offers leadership and teaches young people how to manage their times wisely. He fulfils this command of God:

*"And if thou draw out thy soul to the hungry, and satisfy the afflicted soul; then shall thy light rise in obscurity, and thy darkness be as the noon day: and **the Lord shall guide thee continually**, and satisfy thy soul in drought, and make fat thy bones: and thou shalt be like a watered garden, and like a spring of water, whose waters fail not. And they that shall be of thee shall build the old waste places: **thou shalt raise up the foundations of many generations**, and thou shalt be called, The repairer of the breach, The restorer of paths to dwell in."*

- **ISAIAH 58:10–12**

GODLY FATHERS ESTABLISH GODLY PRIORITIES

My fellow father, living in a manner that will impact the next generation for good requires intentionality and dedication. Do you desire to walk as godly father? Do you want the next generation to rise up and bless you because of the good name you left on earth? Then join me in the crusade to raise the next generation of young people who put God first in all they think and do. Let us make a firm commitment and decision to make the raising of godly children our chief priority in the rest of our lives. How do we achieve this?

I suggest that, first and foremost, let us take on the role of spiritual leadership in your home by being an example of the spiritual disciplines and maturity that you desire to see in your wife and children. As godly fathers, let us assume the primary responsibility for teaching our children Biblical principles, godly character, Scriptural convictions, wise standards, and practical skills. Let us impart good virtues to our children. Let us help our sons unmask their manhood successful under our tutelage.

Let our children see us practically make effort to live right, fight against sin. Let our integrity and living standards serve as good examples to our children. As Christians, let us make time to regularly share God's Word with our family. Teach your children how to read, study, memorize and meditate on the truths of Word of God. Help them identify with Christ's victory and resurrection power and choose to live victorious lives.

As a godly husband, learn to recognize the basic needs of your wife. Do all you can to strengthen your marriage by your attitudes, words, and actions. Maintain communication with your children. Make sure that every son and daughter has adequate training and counsel for the decisions they make. Rearrange your priorities in order to meet the needs of your wife and children, and they will practice same when they grow up and also marry.

Maintain good communication with your parents and parents-in-law. Provide opportunities for them to spend time with your family and reinforce good values. Apply God-honouring principles to finance so that you and your family can experience financial freedom and have more than enough to help children in need. By making good effort to build your life, your relationships, your family, and your vocation on God's principles, you will experience true success.

TAKE RESPONSIBILITY as a man and as a father. When you accept personal responsibility for all of your words, thoughts, actions, attitudes, and motives and ask for forgiveness of those whom you have wronged, you embrace the principle of responsibility in your life. Also, when you entrust your rights and expectations to God and recognize His ownership over all things, you embrace the principle of ownership in your life.

TAKE YOUR CALLING AS A FATHER SERIOUSLY. In your attitudes, words, and actions, help your children understand life. Help them know God and learn the principles of the Word of God (The Bible). These commitments and guiding principles will help you build the solid foundation for a righteous and a godly generation as a father.

ALWAYS REMEMBER THAT, a good father is a: head, source, progenitor, protector, provider, teacher, director, sustainer, leader, mentor, role model and above all, builder of a godly generation. Never forget this, all the rest of the days of your life!

Enjoy fatherhood and keep on offering good fathering! Yes, you can!

BIBLIOGRAPHY

Armin A. Brott, *The Expectant Father*

C. S. Lewis, "The Necessity of Chivalry," *Present Concerns* (New York: Harcourt Brace Jovanovich, 1986)

David Blankenhorn, *Fatherless America* (New York: Basic, 1995).

Dr. Myles Munroe, *The Fatherhood Principle.*

George Gilder, *Men and Marriage* (Gretna, La.: Pelican, 1992).

Margaret Mead, *Male and Female: A Study of the Sexes in a Changing World* (New York: Dell, 1968)

Matthew Bennett, "The Knight Unmasked," *The Quarterly Journal of Military History.*

Meg Meeker, *Strong Fathers, Strong Mothers.*

Renewal as a Way of Life: A Guidebook for Spiritual Growth, by Richard Lovelace, You might also like to read *"The Nature and Nurture of the Soul,"* a free ViewPoint study.

Rex Forehand, *Parenting the String-Willed Child*

Robert Lewis, *Raising A Modern-Day Knight: A Father's Role in GuidingHis Son to authentic Manhood* (Colorado Springs, Colo.: Focus on the Family, 1997)

Will and Ariel Durant, *The Story of Civilization--The Age of Faith 4* (New York: Simon & Schuster, 1950),

ABOUT THE AUTHOR

Richard Akita is an Author, Life Performance Coach and Entrepreneur.

He has four books to his credit, namely:

- ❖ Power of One: *The Starting Point of Infinity,*
- ❖ Every Day in Love, *Inspirational Love Expressions & Insightful Quotes,*
- ❖ *Cheat on Fear,* and
- ❖ *Death of 49(a FREE downloadable Daily Workbook).*

BACKCOVER INFORMATION

HOW DOES A MAN EMBRACE THE CALL OF MANHOOD without compromising the core role in society? In *Unmasking Manhood*, the author points out that, our masculinity is not the question but the function of manhood. According to him, in recognising the difference, an *unmasked man* will embrace the joy and call to being the generator as well as the sustainer of legacy not only in their family but within the community.

Every culture has an expectation of 'man' and their role, yet paradoxically these expectations become the unwritten standard. But in separating the role and function of manhood, 'men' will learn best practices from mentors, coaches, cultures, fathers and heroes. Just imagine the impact we can have on our sons and grandsons!

Richard Akita states, "My journey thus far has been enlightening; a culmination of a great marriage to Najate, mentors, heroes, mistakes and self-discovery has prepared me not only as father to my biological children - Marcelle and Ryzard - but granted me the grace to step into fathering the community and be in readiness for grand parenting."

Wherever you are in your life's journey, read this awesome book, learn great lessons and live well, as you unmask your legacy!

Richard Akita

Richard's *Unmasking Manhood* provides a blueprint for current fathers to learn, adjust and shape their fatherhood performance, whilst offering would-be dads the chance to prepare adequately before starting the journey. Every man must read *Unmasking Manhood!*

Michael Ohene-Effah

A boy graduates into an adolescent and to a man without a training program, yet he is supposed to 'train' his children 'the way' they should 'go'.

Claude A. Mann, Snr

The central argument Richard Akita makes in this book is that manhood is a calling which goes beyond procreating children; he calls for fatherhood as a position of responsibility for men whether they are single, unmarried, divorced, or have their own children.

Emmanuel Kojo Hopeson, PhD

Printed in Great Britain
by Amazon